CHEERS, SPOOK
ENJOY, Sluggo
GO BUFFY

The Sluggo Chronicles

Memoirs of an Old Bomber Pilot

Patrick Daly

Disclaimer: This book reflects the recollections of the author; he has attempted to tell the stories accurately to the best of his knowledge. He assumes no responsibilities for any errors or inconsistencies. Narrative authors are quoted when available. Some names have been omitted or changed when necessary.

INTRODUCTION

Pilots are well known as great story tellers and the stories get better and bolder every time they are told. Over the years, Sluggo was in his prime when telling his flying tales to a willing audience or anyone that would listen. His best friend, Shooter suggested that he should jot some of them down to pass on to family and friends so they wouldn't be forgotten. And so, he began to recall his flying days as a USAF B-52 Stratofortress bomber pilot and write up some of the more outlandish events. Many of the ensuing flying stories were passed on to his cronies, and several were published. The consensus was why don't you compile them into a book and expand the time span to include the early days and your post flying days in the Air Force...and so he did.

Throughout his youth, Sluggo was often defined as playfully rapscallion, moderately fearless but not foolish. When confronted by an obstacle to some possible tomfoolery, he would muse for a time and if it was plausible in his estimation to pull it off without getting caught, his standard saying was "let's do it." This attitude was in effect for much of his formative years and carried over to his Air Force days. He never did anything very bad, but he was frequently on the cusp. He loved his time in the Air Force and flying the magnificent BUFF. Throughout these tales, writer's prerogative and poetic license run amok as some of the hijinks were over 50 years ago. Sluggo has recalled as many details as his aging brain could muster. The specific facts may vary slightly in some cases, and that's fine. The devil's not in the details, it's the story that counts...and in the end the good guys always win.

Dedicated to his beloved Shooter and the BUFF crew dogs that have climbed up the hatch of this ancient beast since 1952 until today...and those that will...until who knows when.

Contents

Chapter One: The Early Days – "Boys Will Be Boys"

What follows are some tales of adventure from and about flying, and the Air Force life of one, Sluggo, originally known as Irish. To establish the base and how it all began, it's important to reflect on the early days. The grandfather of young Irish (the call sign Sluggo had not yet been bestowed) was an engineer and later a senior manager for a major railroad. He would take the young lad for short train rides in the cabs of both diesel and steam engines. The boy proclaimed that he wanted to be a train driver just like grandpa. Gramps said, "no you don't, you should be a pilot and fly airplanes, that's the wave of the future." He bought him a bed for his birthday with a three-foot-long carved wooden propeller on the headboard (Sluggo still has the prop thanks to his baby brother who saved it for him). One of his favorite pastimes was going to the airport to watch the planes. So, the aviation die was cast at an early age. Grandpa was an avid sportsman, hunting, fishing, he did it all and since Irish was the first male grandson, under Gramps tutelage he did too. He even received an engraved shotgun for his first birthday…couldn't lift it much less shoot it. Being from the Pacific Northwest, the love of the great outdoors and the woods was ingrained from youth.

As was the tradition, he attended a private grade school three blocks from home. In grade school he discovered nuns and they discovered him. No very serious altercations but painful lessons learned and quite a few knuckles rapped; they didn't appreciate some of his madcap antics. The nuns liked him, and he liked the nuns but at times he needed physical reminders of who was in charge. He also discovered elementary school tackle football and it became another love…he was small but

spirited…and healed quickly. One particular game comes to mind, his boys were due to play an infamous rival team; the star defensive player of the team was a giant called "Bird Cage." The kid was huge and wore glasses, hence the face mask (a fairly new football safety fixture back in the day) and ergo the nickname. Bird Cage was known to tackle his opponent, fall on him and pinch and grope if the referee wasn't watching. Going up against Bird Cage was the thing of teenage nightmares. The game happened, the legend was true, the boys lost.

Irish received a nifty chemical set from Gramps for his birthday. Back in the day, a good chemistry set could produce numerous compounds including smoke bombs, gun powder, and other pyrotechnic wonders. Also, the corner drug and hardware stores sold other useful potions (not anymore) which could be combined with chemical set materials for amazing results. "This is cool stuff," thought Irish as he conducted yet another exciting new experiment. "Good living through chemistry," quipped Irish as he became more proficient in mixology and things that go boom. Was this a preview of things to come…I wonder?

The neighborhood was classic Norman

GILBERT CHEMISTRY 5

EXPERIMENT I—How to make an explosive mixture

Mix thoroughly 1 measure of sulphur, 1 measure of powdered charcoal and 2 measures of potassium nitrate on glazed paper, but do not grind or rub the mixture. Then put the mixture on an old pan, and, standing off at a suitable distance, out of doors, being careful so as not to burn the hand or face, drop a lighted match on the mixture. Note the sudden flash and puff of smoke. Gunpowder is made from such a mixture, and is probably the longest known explosive. The potassium nitrate acts as an oxidizing agent, evolving oxygen on heating to burn the sulphur to sulphur dioxide and the powdered charcoal to carbon dioxide. *Do not attempt to perform this experiment with proportions of chemicals larger than those stated above.*

Rockwell, big old houses, big yards, plenty of large trees, lots of kids, (Irish was the oldest of seven), hard-working parents and alleys for all the neighborhood brats to hang out, play in, and run wild and act crazy. The surrounding valley was very fertile and truck farms abounded, picking beans and berries was summertime employment for many kids including Irish, (pre-migrant workers times), and the growers depended on the kids. Countless school buses traveled throughout the neighborhoods to ferry the pickers to the fields at the crack of dawn. It was a way to make some money although painful to Irish and most of the guys, the girls however liked it and excelled at picking and making money. Perhaps the boys generally had a bad attitude about being there and so pranks prevailed. The guys' strawberry picking philosophy was pick one, eat one, squeeze one and throw it at the girls, berry stains were indicator of hits…to this day, Irish hates strawberries. The biggest lesson learned from berry and bean picking was to find a real summer job post haste.

As mentioned in the introduction, throughout his youth Irish was often defined as playfully rapscallion, moderately fearless but not foolish. When confronted by an obstacle to some possible tomfoolery, he would muse for a time and if it was plausible in his estimation to pull it off without getting caught, his standard saying would be "hey guys, I've got a plan, let's execute." This description was the truth for much of his formative years. Although the years were filled with many other distractions, his love of airplanes and flight never quit.

It was time to grow, so off to high school. As was the family tradition, Irish attended an all-boys prep school across town, transportation by city bus, and yes, more nuns. The students were organized by testing into Registration Rooms, with Reg 1 being the 50-pound brain guys and so on down, probably not PC today…Irish placed well. The first days of school began with the traditional dog sniffing, quite different from grade school and no girls, repeat no girls, but more nuns. Irish was joined by many old friends and made lots of new friends. Ironically, he was again confronted by the notorious "Birdcage" his real name was Willie, and he was also in the same Reg Room. They soon became close friends, rode to school together, camped and fished together, and got in trouble together. Willie was the culprit that named our boy "Irish" and their friendship continues to this day.

There were big nuns and little nuns and old nuns but no young nuns, and they all knew all the tricks and getting on their bad side was trouble for the perpetrator. Irish and Willie were having too much fun their freshman year and their grades reflected it, so off to summer school to "enrich their programs" in Latin…"Galia est omnis divisa in partes tres"…thanks a load Julius. They passed, in spite of several pranks pulled on the teacher including a fizzie in her morning coffee. But they learned a lesson and grades became more important, Irish even made the National Honor Society his last two years of High School. He also got culture, took Fine Arts and enjoyed it, worked on the class yearbook staff and the class play…was this the madcap Irishman we know and love? Perhaps, but who knows.

And then there was football, JV and Varsity as a pesky linebacker, Irish joined the Letterman Club his last two years, he also got his bell rung more than once. Football became a passion and the school call sign, "the Rams" was an area gridiron powerhouse. Willie was an ace baseball pitcher and didn't do football. So, what to do when there was no football or baseball? Since it was an all-boys school, Irish and Willie became cheerleaders during basketball season…rah rah sis boom bah and flips

and great fun. Irish got a real summer job working in an electroplating plant. He felt right at home with bubbling caldrons of acid and caustics, and electricity arcing, a giant chemistry set. He ended up working there off and on throughout high school and college. Learned plumbing, electrical wiring, welding, chemistry, and other good stuff to be of use in his later years.

Irish got his first car, a 1938 Chevy four door sedan, against his dad's advice that the auto was "too damn old." He immediately got a $29.95 paint job, bright Kelly green. His dad was right, but he kept it running, taking it apart and putting it back together many times. During college it became a party car even featured in parades. He finally sold it for $45. What followed throughout the  years was a cavalcade of weird cars including Hillmans and Sunbeams, he was partial to Brit autos. Irish bought a 52 Chevy convertible for $15. It  had no tires or wheels, the steering was broken, the body and paint were terrible, and the convertible top had multiple holes, but the engine ran well. No problem, buy wheels and tires at the junk yard, weld the steering linkage to the frame forever, iron on patches for the top and many cans of flat black paint all over, and presto, a good car was born and was driven for several years…only leaked during heavy storms. Papa Irish commented several times "the back-yard alley looks like a damn used car lot" …and it probably did. Irish thought perhaps it's time to get rid of some of these beaters, so he did…but he always kept a few around.

Willie, Irish and a couple of other neighborhood guys formed a folk singing group (Kingston Trio like) guitars, banjo and bongos. Originally known as "The Mallards"…bad name…later changed to "The Highlanders"…good name. Irish had no natural musical talent so it was bongos for him. The guys starred in many minor gigs throughout town including fashion shows, fashion shows equal lots of girls. They even cut a commercial for a local pop radio station to the tune of "Michael Row Your Boat Ashore." Speaking of girls, a few minor romances, nothing serious, although Irish thought, "girls are an interesting species and needed to be studied in much more detail." High School was a gas but all good things must come to an end and the four years moved fast. Time for a new experience, college anyone? Scores of his high school cronies, including Willie, were going to attend a small private college in town. Irish joined the crew, got accepted, saved his pennies, secured a student loan and set out for another new life chapter. Something else to think about, the Vietnam War was cranking up and the draft was raising its ugly head…watch out boys!

Chapter Two: College – "Built on a Bluff and Run on the Same Principle"

Young Irish was on his way to matriculate at UP on the bluff, also known as the University of Portland. UP was founded in 1901 and is the sister  school of the University of Notre Dame "Fighting Irish." It is located on a steep bluff overlooking the City of Portland, the Willamette River, Swan Island, the city's first airport now a shipyard (during WW II produced Liberty Ships), and Mocks Bottom. Irish picked Liberal Arts, Political Science as a major, he was a townie not living on campus, but the U was close to his abode. And, by the way, no nun teachers and lots of girls. UP'ers were called the "Pilots" to honor the famed river boat pilots back in the day who would guide ships from the Pacific Ocean to Portland, about 100 miles up the

 Columbia river and down the Willamette River. Very appropriate as Irish's dream of being an aircraft pilot and his love of airplanes had not diminished over the early years. There are very many wonderful stories associated with his time at the U, too numerous to be discussed in this Chronicle, but here's a few special tales.

The U was in a neighborhood known as St. Johns, it was a rough and tumble place of hard-working, manual laborers, nothing beautiful in St. Johns except the suspension bridge spanning the Willamette River to downtown Portland, a  mini Golden Gate. St. Johns was historically a blue-collar neighborhood. It was known for its disparate citizens and its slowly changing appearance. St. Johns was considered one of the city's more diverse and poorest neighborhoods with gangs for all the ethnic groups. Today that has changed with gentrification running wild. Back in the day, taverns were a social focus of the neighborhoods and as such there were two or more on every block on the main drags with names like Your Inn, Blue Bird, Mocks Crest, the Ranger, the Perch and more. Taverns were an interesting Oregon fixture, they served beer and wine only, no hard booze and they were required to serve food of some sort, similar to the pubs in Ireland and England. There was a particular tavern located a few blocks down the road from the campus, naturally it was a student hangout, "The

Twilight Room," better known as The "T Room." Pool tables, Foosball, and lots of tall cool ones, and the food was surprisingly good, the bar's colors, purple and white same as the U's colors...shocker. The T Room was a gathering place for Irish and his townie buddies for many years, and many antics were plotted in its dark recesses...and it's still there.

Air Force Reserve Officer Training Corps (ROTC) was mandatory for guys at the U for their first two years. Irish thought Air Force equals airplanes...I wonder. The AFROTC unit on the campus, known as Detachment 695, was one of the most prestigious and largest in the country. Some of his high school chums were discussing joining the ROTC Drill Team, the Mitchell Rifles, Irish thought no football to play, maybe I'll give that a try... so he did. It was no picnic, lots of hard work at night and weekends and the drill sergeants were always in your face. One guy from Hawaii took special interest in Irish...not in a good way. The team was unique in that they threw rifles with fixed bayonets during their performances. Speaking of rifles, each cadet was assigned his own, responsible for refinishing the wood and keeping the metal shining. The rest of the unique uniform was to be kept spotless at all times and inspections were often. The rifles were real weapons with firing pins removed, relics from both World Wars, Korea and even Vietnam. Today they're still being used by drill teams. "M-1903A3 Breach Loading Magazine Rifle of the Bolt Type, sir." The boys performed as color guards at various events and competed against all the West coast colleges with ROTC drill teams. This involved travelling to different schools, the pinnacle being the annual Western Region Drill Competition including

Army and Navy ROTC drill teams. This year the competition was to be held at Davis-Monthan (DM) Air Force Base in Tucson, Arizona (also known as the "bone yard" where old military airplanes go to die). But how to get the team there, too far for a bus ride. The team advisor and ROTC instructor, an active duty AF Captain and pilot suggested borrowing a Portland Air National Guard aircraft. The Guard, among other airframes flew the C-119 cargo aircraft, also called the "Dollar Nineteen," or the "Flying Boxcar" due to its odd shape. The deal was done, the team would fly to Arizona in a C-119. The aircraft was another relic first flown in 1947

and used extensively in the Korean War, in Vietnam it was even turned into a gunship, over 1,000 were built and flown by numerous countries. The aircraft also starred in the classic movie, "The Flight of the Phoenix." The airplane could carry over 60 troops in the first-class cabin, canvas

web seats on the walls, both sides of the fuselage, comfort guaranteed …but the seat doesn't recline and what's the inflight meal today?

So, let the saga begin. The top speed of the C-119 was 280 kts. with a cruise speed a staggering 200 kts. Distance to DM, around 1,000 miles, estimated flight time nine plus hours. For many of the team including Irish, this was their first flight on a USAF airplane, how impressive… "off we go into the wild blue yonder in a flying boxcar." They departed in a typical Oregon rainstorm, it was either very hot or very cold in the airplane and as they crossed the mountains very turbulent. One of the boys got air sick and the aroma spread throughout the aircraft like the plague and soon a good portion of the guys were ralphing, it didn't bother Irish, a good sign if you want to be a pilot. At last they arrived in time to practice for the big event. They were on their game and won first place in all the competition phases; inspection, standard drill and fancy drill, best in the West beating all the big school teams...take that Army and Navy. A great victory party at the DM NCO/Airman Club, some of the team half in the bag, politely directed back to the Bachelor Officers Quarters (BOQ) by friendly Sky Cops. Soon morning, then back on the "vomit comet" for the ride home.

So, where did the townies hang out when they weren't in class? The answer, The Pilot House. The Pilot House was a commons type building with large rooms, comfortable furniture, tables, chairs, a large fireplace and a snack/burger bar in one end. Many plots were hatched in the Pilot House. Hypothetically speaking, the following might be one of the classics. A bunch of the freshman guys put their heads together to develop

a plan of hijinks for Homecoming festivities which were coming soon. In 1939, two large vintage WW I cannon, a war memorial, were installed on the Bluff pointed  toward the city, overlooking the Swan Island Shipyards, flanked by a large flagpole. The site was used for various ceremonies over the years, it was also a common reference point, "I'll meet you by the cannons at noon." Additionally, they were known as the "Kissin Cannons" after the site became a popular after-hours rendezvous for amorous couples. The plotters determined that one, a 3,147- pound gun with the breach welded shut could be fired old pirate style if a touch hole was drilled. The guys thought this is perfect as the twilight homecoming parade would end near the cannons. They would dress in the hated adversary school colors, come up over the Bluff, throw some flares, scream and yell, fire the cannon and escape and evade over the Bluff. And so, the plan was put in motion.

They drilled out the touch hole, that took about a week, several hours a night (had to run an extension cord from one of the buildings and hide it when the night watchman came around, they also went through many drill bits), mixed several pounds of special homemade gun powder, and prepared various wadding materials. It was decided that it would be too dangerous to load the cannon before the night of the parade so the boys would hide over the Bluff and prepare the shot that night. There would be no projectile only toilet paper and cloth wadding. The boys practiced the operation several times so each culprit would know his job, insert powder and wadding and tamp it all down with a 2X4. The fateful evening arrived and as the homecoming group approached the cannon area, the gang jumped up from the Bluff, did their thing, loaded the cannon and lit the fuse...and nothing, it was a dud. The lads went back over the Bluff to a nearby park for an after-action critique. The chief henchman and explosive mixer was embarrassed, he maintained that the planning and execution were sound, the powder was good...the fuse probably wasn't placed properly. As his pride was at stake, he stated that on the following morning he would insert a new fuse and light it.

Morning came, it was a ROTC drill day, so the culprit was wearing his AF uniform. He didn't have a first period class, so around eight o'clock he made his way to the cannon and inserted a new fuse, after checking the area he lit it. Kaboom, it went off with an ear-splitting blast. Wow, he didn't realize it would be so powerful and loud. There was a moment of total silence, all work at the shipyard stopped, students began coming out of buildings. There was a V of smoldering and burning paper and cloth out to the edge of the Bluff. As people began to form in the area, our slightly deaf cannoneer ran over to the Bluff and

yelled "there were two of them and they jumped over the Bluff, there they go." As people ran over to the edge, he quietly walked away and merged into the crowd. As the campus magazine described later, "the larger cannon was actually fired once, early on a December morning in 1961, as a student prank, rocking the campus with a thunderous jolt." Our boy got away unharmed, although all his buddies knew "who done it," he was never blamed or even questioned and campus life went on. The cannons were quickly filled with concrete, years later they were removed to make way for a new science building. They now reside in American Legion posts. You understand that this was a purely hypothetical story, right...did it happen, what do you think?

There were two men's "social-service clubs" on campus...think fraternities. They were not connected to national organizations and didn't

have frat houses, most of their members were dorm rats. Several of the townies thought there was room for one more organization, they got their act together and briefed the school powers that be. It was approved, and Sigma Tau Omega (STO) was born. After the first growing pains, the initial cadre was ready to take on new members. Irish and Willie and four other gents were asked to be

in the first pledge class, as they knew lots of the members, all good guys, they said yes. Pledging was the usual stuff, blindfold drop-offs at midnight in the weeds with no money, stupid taskings and duties, inane

pledge book entries, you get the idea, but no physical hazing, or maybe just a little. Irish made lots of new friends and rekindled lots of old ones. The other two campus frats didn't think STO would make it, they were wrong, and the original group is still active and in touch today, over 50 years later. In the early 90's fraternities were outlawed at the U citing "their risky behaviors could create serious liability issues and problems for the university." But that was the 90's and we're talking about the mid 60's, not much was politically correct, and a war was going on.

Irish made it through his freshman year at UP, lots of fun, grades not too bad but nothing to write home about. Summer employment at the electroplating plant and some odd jobs at a car dealer, making decent coin. One of the major events of the summer was a gathering of young lads and

lassies at Seaside Oregon over Labor Day weekend. Of historical importance, Seaside was the western most point of the Lewis and Clark expedition. The promenade turn-around at the end of Broadway Street, the main drag, was a monument celebrating their accomplishments. For the past prior years, the celebration got a little bit wild and crazy with thousands of kids doing everything illegal like drinking beer and building fires on the beach, walking down Broadway street blocking traffic, raising hell, and other major crimes. The city fathers and merchants envisioned Seaside as the Martha's Vineyard of the West and this kind of behavior would not be tolerated in the future. The powers that be dubbed the activities a "Riot." It really wasn't a riot in the political sense, it was merely thousands of kids drinking too much beer and raising hell...so I guess you could call it an uprising. So over that Labor Day, they called "all hands on deck," local police, state police, other cops alerted from as far as Portland, 90 miles East, oh and let us alert the fire department and why not the local National Guard, ax handles were the weapons of choice, "these criminals won't get away that kind of behavior this year."

Irish, Willie, and a handful of friends from the U and other pals, decided to make the trip to Seaside on Labor Day, headquarters would be a beach house owned by Willie's girlfriend's parents. They met up with some other Portland cronies and soon the festivities began, playing games on the beach, catching some rays, drinking beer, checking out the girls, you get the idea. Daylight was waning, and as the story goes, there was a fight on the beach near the promenade and the cops came in with ax handles swinging. The kids didn't like it much and soon thousands were assembling and moving onto Broadway, as the cops were outnumbered, they retreated and called in the backups. Irish and crew joined the mob simply to observe the goings on. As the reinforced phalanx charged the kids with ax handles swinging, Irish became separated from Willie and the group.

About this time several events were transpiring, the rioters moved the 30-foot lifeguard stand up on the promenade and started to roll it down the main drag. The fire department arrived with a pump truck and began hosing down the troops; as three or four firemen directed the nozzle some smart individual made his way to the undefended fire engine, turned off the ignition, removed the keys and fled. As the water pressure dwindled, the firemen looked around fearing the mob would tear them limb from limb, the group broke out in hilarious laughter and the firemen fled. Several windows were broken, and the mob began throwing beer

bottles at the cops. Irish thought it's time to get the hell out of here but he needed to cross the street. As he ran, our hero was whacked on the head by an ax handle swinging fireman and it was lights out for Irish. Off to the Seaside jail with over 200 of his new friends and a lump on his head. About 40 of his fellow inmates were crammed into a cell made for four. Many were in various phases of drunken stupors praying to the single pot bolted to the floor and other disgusting things...no further description required or necessary. Irish thought I'm here for the night and hopefully my friends will figure out I'm in here and come and bail me out, so I'll find a corner to sit down and try to sleep.

The normal bail in Seaside for "disturbing the peace" was $54.50 not a problem for his pals to pass the hat but when they tried to get him out, the bail for the offense was now $504.50 and the charge was "inciting to riot." This far exceeded the capability of his buddies, so it was time to get father Irish, Pete involved. Needless to say, Pete was pissed with the whole situation. In the morning he called a well-known ex-classmate lawyer who in turn called Seaside to get the details; they only had Irish's name from his driver's license, and no other information – where was he, what was he doing, who arrested him, how did he get to jail. They did say that he was one of the sober ones. Pete made the trip to Seaside and got him out. Irish explained that he wasn't rioting (which was true, he wanted to make love not war), but he was in the wrong place at the wrong time. To make a long story short, since the cops didn't have any information on Irish and he had an attorney, all charges were dropped, but Pete was still pissed big time. Irish found out years later that one of his future STO brothers was in the cell next to him.

When the dust had cleared, the mayor of Seaside proclaimed that college-age students would "not be welcome in Seaside" anymore, insisting he would prevail upon local hotels and motels to refuse them rooms. As the Portland newspaper later reported, "That plan backfired, and a new tradition was born. Young ruffians returned to Seaside the following Labor Day weekend, and the one after that, kicking up new riots each time. A massive show of force by National Guardsmen and state troopers finally put an end to the annual disturbances in the middle of the decade." Thirty-five years later, Seasiders experienced an unexpected blast from the past. In March of 1999, "a crowd of mostly young people rioted downtown, at the start of Oregon schools' Spring Break." The Seaside incident continued to haunt Irish for many years as all Federal Security Clearance Investigations asked the question "have you ever been arrested, where, when, and why?" The Seaside jail is now the Seaside Brewing Co, a brewpub – how fitting.

The fraternity was a welcome retreat from the daily grind but with no devoted turf, it was necessary to rent halls for large meetings. There were several venues available for rent at modest fees, Granges, Oddfellows, Vets, you get the idea. These meetings were usually accompanied by a keg or so of beer for the social portion and, as women were not always invited, at times they often became quite boisterous. One particular meeting was a classic. The boys were down in a semi basement and all was well. One of the guys noticed that the meeting room above was populated by a group of neo-Nazis complete with brown shirts, swastikas and even a few wearing jack boots. As more beer was consumed someone suggested since they had lots beer, "let's invite the Hitler guys down for a few and see what they're up to." To make a long story short they never had an empty glass and some of them were becoming sloshed. They talked one into making a speech standing on a chair. As he orated the guys filled his jackboots with beer...he either didn't care or didn't feel it.

While we're discussing beer, there were some local favorites – Blitz Weinhard and Olympia, now both deceased...but only in stubbies please.

Alas, stubbies were phased out in the 80's for the long necks…is there no justice. In 1862, Henry Weinhard a German immigrant moved to Portland and built a brewery occupying two full blocks downtown. The brewery was a fixture of an old industrial and warehouse district, now the yuppie Pearl district. The big brewers snapped Blitz up in the late 90's. Leopold Schmidt, another German, founded The Capital Brewing Company at Tumwater Falls on the Deschutes River in the town of Tumwater, near Olympia, the Capitol of Washington State. He began brewing and selling Olympia Beer in 1902, with the classy hook "It's the Water." As with Blitz the big guys snatched it too. Another favorite was the potent elixir "Big Cat" some of the guys maintained that if you drank too much of the "malt licker" the tiger would jump off the can and attack you.

Sauvie Island is the largest island along the Columbia River at 26,000 acres, and one of the largest river islands in the United States. It's about ten miles from downtown Portland, between the Columbia River to the east, the Multnomah Channel to the west, and the Willamette River to the south. Most of the 32 square mile island is designated as a wildlife area. The middle of the island contains numerous small  truck farms growing all kinds of crops including the despised strawberry. Most of the coastlines are public beaches (now including a clothing optional area). Many STO ceremonies, fishing, basking and beer drinking were held on Sauvies, close to the campus and back in the day, wide open, wet, wild, and wonderful.

Man has always been captivated by the moon and its varied phases including the mooning phase, the boys of STO were no exception. Officially, *"mooning* is the act of displaying one's bare buttocks by removing clothing, e.g., by lowering the backside of one's trousers and underpants, and usually bending over."   The   Oxford   English Dictionary dates mooning to student slang of the 1960s, when the gesture became   increasingly   popular   at American universities. It was the sign of the times, usually a sign of affection and good will...sure.

There are many mooning stories, too numerous to be discussed here. Butt, one of the most significant mooning legends involved our boys and Sauvies Island. If you recall, although 100 miles from the ocean, Portland was a deep draft port used by numerous ocean-going vessels who would

cruise by Sauvies on their way to unload. One sunny afternoon the gang was involved in a beer infused attitude check on the Island. As the ships made their   way   by   Sauvies, someone suggested that the crew   of   an   Asian freighter passing by after their long journey might appreciate a multiple moon. And so it came to pass and soon the ship's crew was lining the rails and cheering the crazy Americans.

The fraternity was active in other events around campus. The Federal Government was annexing entire neighborhoods near the U to construct the Interstate 5 border to border freeway. Vast amounts

of broken concrete were stacked during the process. The current pledge class decided to build a concrete "P" on the side of the Bluff with the scrap material. They commandeered an old Army dump truck from the U and the work began and it was no easy task. The group engineers did the planning and the recommendation was a 70-foot high letter. And so, the trial began, fighting the slope, poison ivy and oak, and bugs and critters. At last it was finished, cemented in and white-washed, and a grand edifice it was. Alas, over the years with the demise of STO the "P" has fallen into disrepair. Nothing that a little whitewash couldn't fix…and it's still there…quite an engineering feat.

Many parties followed, always great, homecoming, parades, and sponsored campus dances to mention a few. One such dance featured a

jungle motif; someone came up with the idea of renting a gorilla suit to advertise the event. Off to a professional costume rental shop downtown. The suit was beyond all expectations although the owner was worried it would get damaged, after promising their first born and other concessions the lady said OK. What followed was a week of serious hijinks and tomfoolery, you can't imagine the fun you can have with a real looking gorilla suit, raging through dining facilities, dorms and other venues. The "T" Room and other taverns, downtown Broadway, and

various lover's parking retreats…it's a wonder no one was shot.

There were some serious moments in this madcap activity. Irish had to make the decision to commit the next two years to the AFROTC program. That included a month-long Summer Camp which was a glorified "Boot Camp" conducted at an Air Force Base in the San Francisco Bay area, not a lot of fun but a necessary evil. A few weekends in wild and crazy North Beach anyone?

As the years sped by, his love of airplanes never quit. At summer camp, Irish got an initiation flight in the back seat of a F101, Voodoo interceptor. The Voodoo was a two-engine supersonic go-fast jet, top speed 1,000 mph plus, "I could get used to this" thought Irish. One of the STO guys was from the area, his parents invited all over for a little BBQ, the house was on a channel with a boat in the back yard, very nice, and the touch of home was greatly appreciated.

Off to his senior year and flying. He had been accepted in the Flight Introduction Program (FIP) which included ground school and 40 hours of flight training culminating in a Private Pilot License. The subject airplane was a Piper Colt, about as simple a flying machine as one could find. Fixed tricycle landing gear, no flaps, high wing, and a stunning 108 hp 4 banger engine. Spins and stalls, touch and go landings, instrument flying under the bag (one peek is worth a thousand crosschecks), cross country navigation, night flying, emergency procedures, they did it all. He got his license and spent every available dollar renting airplanes and flying. He flew whenever he could or when he could split the cost with anyone crazy enough to go with him.

One day he cornered Willie and said, "let's go flying," and they did. When Willie got home, his mother Lois asked him what he did today. "Went flying with Irish," was the response. "Are you nuts?" was the reply. Another day, Irish flew down to the Oregon coast. On his way back North he was flying the highway, looked down and discovered to his chagrin that the cars on the road were going faster than he was…headwind anyone? Irish managed to get checked out in four different type air machines and amass over 60 more hours. A favorite trick was buzzing the college campus especially in the summer to catch the girls sunning on the dorm roof (no co-ed dorms in those days.) After numerous incidents, the ROTC Professor of Aerospace Studies called him into his office and chewed his ass. The Colonel stated, "if you buzz this campus

one more time that's the end for you, no commission and no pilot training.

He saw the light instantly and strafing the campus was over. Soon it was time for graduation, commissioning as a USAF Second Lieutenant butter bar, and anxiously awaiting military orders to Undergraduate Pilot Training (UPT). The U of P was and still is a great school, and Irish savored every moment (almost) of that experience.

Chapter Three: Undergraduate Pilot Training – "Slipping the Surly Bonds in a Jet"

After graduation from college, commissioning in the USAF and selection for pilot training, Irish had several months to wait before a slot opened at UPT. He could either go on active duty in casual status and count wieners in a mess hall somewhere or delay entry. He decided to wait and worked in a foundry pouring molten aluminum by day and tending bar in a tavern by night (you're never a stranger at the Ranger) and flying whenever he could afford it. At last his orders came, Williams AFB in the Arizona desert, considered by many to be the best UPT base. 2nd Lt. Irish packed his Studebaker Grand Turismo Hawk and departed for Willy Air Patch. He arrived, reported in a military manner and proceeded to the BOQ about 30 yards across the parking lot from the Officers Club, (O'Club), to a 2-bedroom suite which he shared with a guy from North Dakota, call sign "Nogs". The proximity to the O'Club was both a good and bad thing…go figure.

The following day, they assembled at the Club for orientation, which went something like this "Welcome to the year of 53 weeks, this will be the most intense training any of you have ever experienced. Look to your right then look to your left, chances are the guys sitting next to you won't make it through the program," —and so it started. 79 eager aviators including 11 German Air Force (Luftwaffe) students divided into two flights. The year-long ordeal began, twelve plus hour days, academics, physical training (PT), physiological training and yes, flying. And great adventures like being shot 50 feet up in the air in an ejection seat trainer called the "boom bucket" with a blank cannon shell under your butt. When it was our hero's turn to ride the boom bucket, he assumed the proper position, rotated the handles, and squeezed the

triggers and nothing happened. The instructors yelled "don't move, stay in the ejection position and don't do anything." They disarmed the contraption, got Irish out of the seat, no harm, no foul and life was good. Lots of parachute training followed, suspended agony, parachute landing falls (PLFs), let's jump out of towers, bruises and bruises after parachute landings in the cacti infested desert, burr in the ass anyone? Water survival…intentional drowning. Altitude chamber, how long does it take until your fingernails turn blue?

Aerodynamics, navigation, systems, instruments, weather, you get the idea. And lots and lots of PT, including a very odd game called flickerball…playing basketball with a football…strange. And finally, let us go fly.

Phase one of the flying began with a long AF blue bus ride to a civilian airfield where the boys would fly the Cessna 172, known in the USAF as the T-41. The plan was to aviate with some crusty old civilian instructors who probably flew biplanes back in the day…they would see if you had the right stuff or not. This was a serious weeding out process

as most of the class had never piloted an airplane. There was a significant washout rate mostly for air sickness and self-initiated elimination (SIE) or second thoughts about flying after a few dozen unusual attitudes and spins. Irish thought this pilot training is going to be a breeze as I already have my civilian license…boy was he in for the shock of his life. A few others had flown before, including the Germans as well as some AF Academy guys and the student leader, a Captain navigator who had been a back seater in F-101s. Graduation from T-41s included being tossed into a cattle watering tank when you soloed. Next stop, T-37s and no blue bus ride.

Transitioning into T-37's, Irish's class became 67F "No Loss" Flight. The Cessna T-37 was a small two engine jet trainer. Top speed 425 mph, ceiling 35,000 ft. T/O weight 6,569 lbs., ejection seats, oxygen, and…I, repeat and, side by side seating where the instructor pilot (IP) could get his hands on you…as if that would ever happen. Its nickname  was the "Tweety Bird" or for short the "Tweet" because of the high-pitched scream that it made whenever the engines were running. Often called "The Converter" …the airplane that converts jet fuel to noise and "the 6,000-lb. dog whistle." But it was a great airplane with no frills or automatic anything…great for formation and acrobatics. Home for Irish for the next 90 flight hours. On his first flight, Irish was so far behind that his instructor asked him if he was wearing a jock…he said "no" and the  instructor said, "I thought not, if you were it would still be back on the ground." "This is not going to be as easy as I thought it would be, in fact it's damn hard," mused Irish.

The Tweet was famous for the way it performed in a spin. As one student (stud) summed it up, "the plane also had a spin recovery procedure so complicated that most student pilots could barely remember the boldface verbatim items while sitting at the briefing table—let alone in the actual jet while you were hurtling towards your death in a spin with an instructor screaming at you just one foot from your face." Most of the airplanes were so bent from spinning that it took large amounts of trim to make them fly straight, but it was a strong machine, built like a tank.

Since it was a tandem cockpit and the instructor could get his paws on you, some of the gang received unscheduled airborne physical training. A favorite IP trick was grabbing the studs' oxygen mask hose and giving the lad a big head shake to make the point. Irish had a great instructor, an easy going southern boy who pulled him through without screaming or laying on of hands. Again, washouts and SIEs, some just couldn't fly the Tweet in unusual attitudes without getting airsick. So solo, pass your final check ride, then transition to the T-38. The Tweet was so tough that the AF slapped some bigger engines on it, a gun, and bomb racks and sent it to Vietnam as a ground attack bird.

After transitioning into T-38's, Irish's class became 67F "Tipper" Flight, the patch depicted a playboy bunny tipping a martini glass... that would never float today. The Northrop T-38 "Talon" was <u>the</u> machine...it looked like it was going fast just sitting on the ground. The T-38 went like a rocket, two turbojets with afterburner. Top speed, supersonic, Mach 1.3/ 858 mph, ceiling 50,000 ft., rate of climb an amazing 33,600 ft. per minute. In fact, in 1962 it set four time to climb world records. It was a direct descendent of the

F-5 fighter. Its nickname was "the white rocket," home for Irish for the next 120 flight hours. If the T-37 could get your jock, the T-38 could wash and iron it...what a jet.

Irish and four other studs sat at one table to mission plan together with lots of "there I was" hand signals... then alternately fly with their 1st

Lieutenant IP, a rather cocky and arrogant individual, call sign "the Prince." The 38 had tandem seating with the IP in the back seat and the stud in the front, different from the 37 where the IP and Stud could converse

normally, the only way the IP could talk was through the intercom system, also he couldn't get paws on you, although with a rapid aileron roll he could bang your helmet against the canopy. The Prince was known as a screamer..."better teaching through shrieking." Although it was impossible, as the story went you could hear the Prince yelling even though the interphone was turned off. Irish thought "times are going to be tough flying with the Prince"…and they were.

The jet was amazing and flew like a dream, four ship formation, loops, aileron rolls so fast you could hardly do just one, pitch outs and rejoins, barrel rolls…fighter stuff, you get the idea. But no practice spins in the T-38…the emergency procedure for a flat spin recovery was "bailout." And then there was the G-suit, "an anti-gravity garment worn by fighter pilots. When they are pulling positive G's, the suit inflates and prevents blood from pooling in their feet and legs which would cause them to lose consciousness" and a place to put your flight gloves and look cool while strutting around on the ground. Irish had no fun with

instruments until the light finally went on, but he was an ace at formation. It all led up to flying solo by yourself in the jet, a true rite

of passage and how badly can you really scare yourself. Finally, you were the senior class proudly wearing the T-38 solo patch on the flight suit and awaiting the dreaded final check ride.

Since the flight was "Tipper" with the playboy bunny on the patch, the real playboy bunnies from the big city invited the guys to their club and the bunnies were invited out to the base for photo ops with the T-38s and the guys…not too shabby, and even a few romances evolved.

There are many UPT tales, here's a couple. One of the boys, call sign "Count" was from quite a wealthy family. His tailored uniforms were the finest, including a sword and a cape for his formal "Mess Dress." In front of the O'Club were two reserved parking spots side by side; one was designated for the Wing Commander with a large eagle, the other for "any 2nd Lieutenant" with a large gold "butter bar." The Wing King had just purchased a new revolutionary auto, the Oldsmobile Tornado, designated "the car of the year" and "ahead of its time" and proudly parked it in his spot. Not to be out done, the Count went to town and bought a fancier Tornado and of course parked it next to the Colonel who remarked "Who's car is that...some 2nd lieutenant's?" When told yes, he cracked up laughing, ... a good guy...it could have turned out badly for the Count.

One of the German students was stopped by the sheriff for going supersonic on the highway going back to the base, a notorious speed trap. At a flight meeting, their Training Officer (TO)...a hard ass old Captain with no sense of humor who probably wasn't too happy babysitting a bunch of butter bars...asked him why he got the ticket and in a typical serious Germanic tone he replied, "because I had to slow down for the bridge Sir" ...no one had the stones to laugh and the Captain didn't quite know what to do as the guy was dead serious.

Concerning the Captain and Irish, it was love at first sight, the TO thought "this Irish guy is a smart ass...he's in my gunsight." Irish thought "this TO is a real dick, I'd better watch my step." First impressions proved to be accurate, and Irish became the subject of numerous administrative bombs...quarters inspections, PT gear on the floor, one minute late for

class, a parking ticket, and other BS infractions. He became an expert on Reply by Indorsements (RBIs). "The RBI is a military letter sent by an instructor to a student who must respond, in writing, as to circumstances relating to an action which the student took and should not have or did not take and should have. The RBI is intended primarily to be used as a teaching device, though it may also serve other functions" "other functions like harassment," mused Irish, "but this jerk is not going to get me." He became such an expert at answering RBIs, that all the guys sought his expertise when they got one. When the beloved TO moved on to another job, his replacement was a super guy, life was good and no more RBIs for Irish.

Tipper Flight was selected to perform as window dressing and extras in a Hollywood motion picture produced for the Air Force complete with no fooling real actors (one star was a young Mike Farrell of MASH fame) portraying the trials and tribulations of UPT. Since most of the guys were bachelors they had to recruit "wives" from other flights for the social family shoots. What a

The Year of 53 Weeks
USAF Supersonic Pilot Training

hoot, got the boys out of PT for a while, dance with some other guy's wife, and eat free food. (You can still find the movie on YouTube titled, *The Year of 53 Weeks).*

Time flies and so did the guys, and soon the fateful days were here, final check rides...you bet your wings and a few wash backs. After passing the final check ride, the question of the year, where am I going, what am I going to fly...of course most of the class wanted fighters...and then the assignments came down. Of the 38 guys they started with a year ago, only 25 were left, the Germans, Academy guys, the Captain, and 17 lowly 2nd Lieutenants, "that was one damn tough year," Irish thought.

He graduated, pinned on his wings, and got his dream job...the back seat of an F-4 fighter. But not so fast future aces, before leaving town, the boys were called in and informed that most of them would not be going to F-4's as the Air Force was now beginning to put navigators in that position, better known as GIBs (guys in back). A few of the top guns got fighters and the aircraft of their choice, the rest had had to choose between

Caribous (a small two engine transport that the AF had stolen from the Army), KC-135 tankers, or B-52s, all as copilots. Irish figured the B-52 had guns and dropped bombs (he was always partial to explosives) so off he went to the Strategic Air Command (SAC) to learn to fly the BUFF (Big Ugly Fat Fellow)...Fellow to some but something else to others.

PostScript..."No loss/Tipper" also known as "F-Troop" celebrated their USAF Undergraduate Pilot Training 50th reunion in Washington DC. Of the 25 that graduated, five had slipped the surly bonds of earth, one lost in combat. 14 of the remaining group attended including two of their German brothers. A truly great time was had by all, the war stories abounded, the MIGs were buzzing around them like flies on poop, and the flack was so thick you could walk on it.

Chapter Four: Arc Light One – "A Copilot's Lament and Midnight Golf on Guam"

As discussed, our boy was off to SAC to learn to fly the BUFF. First to Nuclear Weapons School in Texas, then Survival School in the deep woods outside Spokane, Washington (not too tough for a guy from the Pacific Northwest, however the POW camp was no fun) then several months of B-52 School in California. Irish was lucky, at BUFF school the student crew was usually made up of a student aircraft commander (pilot) and two student copilots but in their case, there was no student pilot, so three copilots shared the work on all the missions. The instructor was a good guy and said "I'm going teach you boys all the stuff that a student pilot would get including low level, air refueling, pattern work, and touch and go landings"…and he did. Irish loved and excelled at formation flying at UPT so at air refueling he was a natural. By graduation time he could air refuel fairly well, which was unusual for a rookie copilot. Then at last off to Fairchild AFB as a newly minted B-52 D model copilot (the D model was the workhorse of the SAC bombing campaign in Southeast Asia).

At Fairchild he started the exhausting process of becoming SAC-cumsized as a Combat Crew member, serious business. His first flight at the base was with a grizzled old Lt Col WW II and Korea former B-29 pilot. Irish was running the preflight checks and belting out the challenge and response checklist as he was taught but he was getting no answers from the pilot. After he repeated items several times, the pilot said "I'll do all my stuff over here and you do all your stuff over there, tell me when you're done"… and so his life as copilot began.

Irish became Combat Ready in no time and joined his first crew. They were a good bunch of guys; the navigator, call sign "Ponse" was also new and he and Irish became fast friends (and still are to this day). Soon he was on his first

nuclear alert tour, more about alert later. His first aircraft commander

from Walla Walla, Washington, was pleasantly surprised when he discovered Irish could refuel and land. It wasn't long before the crew was informed that they would soon be deploying to Southeast Asia (SEA) for operation "Arc Light" (the designation for SAC's SEA bombing campaign). So off again to B-52 school for conventional bombing training and then to Guam.

1st Lt Irish (he was promoted) met lots of his UPT/BUFF school copilot buddies on Guam. Over some beers one night at the O Club, they discussed the fact that all the colonels had radio call signs; Alpha, Bravo, Charlie, Uncle Ned, et.al. So, the boys decided that they would all acquire call signs so they could talk to each other on the radio without being identified. So, Basie, Mack, Cash, Sluggo and other call signs were born (the guys thought Irish resembled the character in the Nancy and Sluggo cartoon, so the name). If a multiple aircraft departure went exceptionally well, many times Alpha (the Wing King) would congratulate Charlie on the launch over the radio. So, after one launch, Sluggo decided he would also congratulate Charlie, "Charlie this is Sluggo, nice launch" and Charlie responded "Thanks Sir" as he probably fumbled with his code book to try to figure out who the hell Sluggo was.

It was May 1968, about 1700 Guam time. Sluggo was part of a six aircraft formation that had just landed at Andersen from a 12-hour plus bombing mission in Vietnam. One of his copilot buddies announced that the drinks were on him as he had just been selected for Captain. The plan was to clean up and catch the shuttle bus to the Officers Club for a celebration (a shuttle bus ran from the BOQ compound to the club and back on about the half hours). As nobody was scheduled to fly for two days...a "horror show" was definitely in order.

A wonderful time was had by all including many toasts, several rounds of "Carrier Landings", a few "Dead Bugs", and some "Flaming Hookers". Sluggo and five or six of his copilot cronies closed the club down near midnight and staggered out to the shuttle bus for the ride back to the BOQ. When they got on the bus, the driver was quite disturbed, he advised them that as of midnight he was no longer in the Air Force and he wasn't working one second past midnight, his flight home was all screwed up, it wasn't fair, and on and on he ranted. He said he was going directly back to the motor pool without stopping and "was tired of driving you drunk officers back to the BOQ every night"…everyone cheered and laughed and off they went to the motor pool which was less than mile from the BOQ compound.

When they arrived at the motor pool the driver shut down the bus and ran into the building. The boys observed a B-52 tug (Military Aircraft Tug, Tow Tractor) with no driver, idling at the curb in front of the motor

pool. As you can see, they are rather large and powerful machines. One of the guys said, "I know how to drive one of those beauties, and I also believe that's our transportation back to the BOQ." They all agreed, jumped on and away they went in a cloud of diesel smoke.

The road to the BOQ paralleled several of the fairways on the Base Golf Course. The boys had only gone a couple of blocks when they observed several Air Police vehicles in hot pursuit with lights flashing and sirens blaring. Apparently, the tug driver, who went into the motor pool for a quick relief, discovered his vehicle missing and called the Air Police on the pool's hot line.

The tug was no sports car and at single digit MPH's no land speed records were in jeopardy and the police were quickly closing the gap. So, the guy driving yelled "hang on we're going to escape and evade" as he turned off the road over the curb and onto the golf course fairway. The sky cops hesitated for a moment and then followed; soon the guys were running out of real estate and approaching the jungle on the other side of  the fairway. The driver yelled "we're stopping, every man for himself!" He hit the brakes and the boys jumped off and made for the jungle. Lt Sluggo headed out at a dead run losing a shoe in the process and entered the jungle looking for a place to hide. The cops were close in trail shining flashlights and yelling stop. Lt. Sluggo spotted a cluster of small trees with low limbs and thought "if I climb up there maybe they won't spot me" he climbed up on the limbs and watched as the cops searched the area.

Apparently, Lt Sluggo decided to call it a night in the tree and fell into a deep sleep (stupor)…he was awakened as the sun was coming up. Aside from ample bug bites and one missing shoe and a headache he was in pretty good shape. He climbed down, looked around, got his bearings and started to walk back to the BOQ pretty full of himself realizing he'd managed not to get caught. But as he crested a slight hill in the fairway, he observed a number of Air Police patrolling on the other side. He tried to duck back below the hill, but the cops had spotted him. "Lt Sluggo, we know it's you, the gigs up, come out" blared over a megaphone. Sluggo was taken into custody and hustled off to the police station. When he asked the cops "How did you know it was me?" they replied "We caught the rest of your buddies and turned them over to their aircraft commanders, by process of elimination and the fact that your bed hadn't been slept in, and that they were all your friends, we figured out that the other crook was you. You'll be happy to know, none of your cronies ratted you out."

Shortly after he was booked, his aircraft commander came to the station and picked him up. He said, "The squadron commander wants to see you ASAP, so go clean up put on a uniform and get your ass to his office." So, he did, the squadron commander asked him, "What the hell were the boys were thinking about by stealing a government vehicle, especially a tug?" He then presented him a letter of reprimand and told him to clean up his act. The letter read like this "You are hereby reprimanded for your conduct on the night of 29 May 1968 when you were apprehended by the Andersen AFB Base Patrolmen and charged with misappropriation of a government vehicle. The seriousness of this charge cannot be over emphasized nor can conduct of this nature be tolerated in the future."

A day later when the crew was preparing to fly their next mission; the pre-mission briefing included a viewgraph cartoon depicting a guy in a flight suit at the top of a coconut palm tree with an Air Police car and a cop with a megaphone below telling him to come down. A thunderous laugh went through the flight crews and briefers including even a few colonels as word of the episode had gotten around. Lt Sluggo was contrite but relieved that perhaps the incident wasn't as serious as he thought. Several months later his squadron commander gave him the unsigned letter of reprimand which never again saw the light of day. He later received an outstanding grade on his escape and evasion techniques from his copilot buddies. He never found the missing shoe.

The Arc Light missions rotated between bases in Andersen AFB, Guam, Kadena AB, Okinawa, and Utapao RTNB Thailand. The crew dogs spent around a month in each place then moved on to the next. Each base had its own uniqueness and of course, the accompanying specific hijinks and tall tales. An individual Chronicle chapter will be devoted to each venue. After 179 action packed days of "Arc Light," Lt Sluggo returned to the real world.

Chapter Five: Nuclear Alert – "How I Learned to Love the Bomb"

As previously discussed, Sluggo attended nuclear weapons school prior to departing to his first base as a B-52 C/D model copilot. Upon arriving, he started the grueling process of becoming combat ready. Study, testing, more testing, more studying on the Single Integrated Operations Plan (SIOP), or the checklist on how to go to nuclear war, God forbid should the task arise. Then formal oral and written testing... until error free, no busts allowed. SAC was a serious taskmaster, no margin for mistakes "to err is human...to forgive is not SAC policy." And then into the "Mole Hole" on nuclear alert.

Nuclear alert was no kidding, somber business...well maybe there was some kidding at times. The "Mole Hole", which was next to the 'Christmas Tree" was the semi-underground facility where the well-fed

alert crew dogs lived for their usually 24/7 tour followed by three days off. The "Christmas Tree" was the parking area for the on-alert BUFFs. Alert crews lived in the bottom of the mole hole with ramps leading out to the Christmas Tree; chow hall, rec rooms, offices, security, and other stuff were located on the top level.

The usual alert configuration for the alert aircraft was four B28 thermonuclear bombs in a clip-in assembly in the BUFF bomb bay. The

B28 was a dial-a-yield weapon; kilotons up to one plus megaton. Over the years of airborne alert, a few were involved in accidents, one of the most infamous is perhaps "the rain in Spain" where a bomber and a tanker collided and four B28's were strewn over Spanish land and sea...all recovered, dirty radiological release but no nuclear yield. Some alert bombers also carried two AGM-28 nuclear tipped Hound Dog missiles under the wings...they were the father of the modern cruise missile... jet powered and notoriously inaccurate and difficult to program. As the story goes, after launch the missile will hit the ground somewhere (the circular error probability

was over two miles) but they were nukes, so what the hey. Sexy to look at, but also the bane of all BUFF copilots.

The missile engine controls were owned by the copilot and the aircraft fuel panel, also owned by the copilot, was used to transfer fuel

from the BUFF to the Hell Dogs (copilots unflattering name for the missiles) and keep them full of gas while their engines were running during a simulated launch (a royal pain). One of Sluggo's copilot buddies was flying a no notice check ride with missiles (serious business), he was doing a truly sterling job and acing it, after landing he was feeling quite full of himself until after BUFF engine shutdown when the evaluator asked him "what's that noise" and yes, he had forgotten to shut down the Hell Dog's engines. The book said that the missile engines could also be used for takeoff, but Sluggo never heard of or saw that happen..."we got our eight good buddies running...why screw with the Hell Dogs, they're nothing but trouble and their intakes are so low to the ground just begging to suck up crap and FOD off the taxi ways and runway" (FOD – AF speak for foreign object damage).

So Sluggo began his first copilot alert tour, standard procedures were an official turnover briefing with the outgoing crew including signing a "hand receipt" for the nuclear weapons...no kidding, and then the incoming crew doing a preflight of the alert bird. Off to the airplane in the SAC blue alert truck. Upon arriving at the airplane, the pilot asked Sluggo for the airplane key, he said, "What sir, I don't have any key." The pilot said, "Lieutenant you don't think we'd leave this B-52 unlocked with all the nukes on board do you...didn't anyone tell you it's your job to pick up the alert key?" Sluggo was stumped until he saw the rest of the crew laughing...he'd been had, there was no BUFF key, and alas the first chapter of future alert humor for Sluggo was written.

There were four levels of exercising on alert, all no notice, the klaxon could blow any time day or night for an *Alpha*, proceed to the aircraft, copy message, authenticate, acknowledge. For a *Bravo*, proceed to the aircraft, copy message, authenticate, acknowledge and start engines. BUFFs were equipped with explosive (gun powder like) cartridges (about the size of a 2 lb. coffee can) on two engines enabling a start with no external support from all the stuff painted yellow that usually surrounds an airplane when parked. They made quite a cloud of smoke when fired. Later Buffs were modified with a cartridge on all eight motors to cut down reaction time, when first fired they made so much smoke that the ground crew was nearly gassed, and the tower thought the aircraft was on fire.

But back to alert modes; for a *Charlie*, proceed to aircraft, copy message, acknowledge, authenticate, start engines, and taxi simulating a wartime launch, also called a Coco exercise or more appropriate, an elephant walk...it took many hours to recover and get back to normal nuclear alert following a Coco after a slew of bombers and tankers were scattered all over the ramp and taxiways (all still basically on alert). And finally, for a *Delta*, do the above and launch on airborne alert. Sluggo never saw a true *Delta* as SAC airborne alert was canceled before Sluggo's time (Operation Chrome Dome, 1960-1968, nuke armed BUFFs in the air 24/7/365). Sluggo did launch once in a B-52 C with weapons on a modified airborne alert, after three air refuelings and 23 1/2 hours of boring holes in the arctic sky, they landed...SAC launched only a couple of aircraft on this mission, and for only a couple of days before recalling...the boys were never really told why or for what.

Some less than serious alert moments come to mind. The B-52 (except the H model) used a water injection system to increase engine thrust on takeoff, especially vital for the alert birds which were fully loaded to maximum takeoff gross weight (models C thru F 450,000 lbs., G&H 488,000 lbs.). The older BUFFs carried 1200 gallons of de-mineralized water in a tank behind the cockpit, it would provide a boost on takeoff for 110 seconds, Sluggo wondered how does one increase engine power by dumping water into it, but hey, I'm just a dumb copilot. Water, 32 degrees, Northern tier AFB what does that add up to…water in your BUFF might freeze…not good. Normal alert procedure, when the weather met certain parameters, the water needed to be drained. The water dump was located on the copilot's side/near top of the fuselage.

On one of Sluggo's first alert tours conditions dictated dumping water. One night, Sluggo's Aircraft Commander (AC) said, "let's go drain the water" and off they went in company of the navigator. After they got power on the aircraft the pilot said, "Sluggo go outside and visually check that the water is draining properly." "Yes sir," said Sluggo and away he went although he had no idea what he was supposed to be looking for. With Sluggo gazing up, the pilot hit the drain switch…to say that the results were similar to a cow and a flat rock was putting it mildly…alas, a soggy Sluggo was had again, another character-building chapter in the alert experience.

Talking about winter alert at the Northern tier, the first significant snowfall guaranteed a crew dog snowball fight both outside and inside the mole hole after the heavies called it a day. Only problem was getting the place cleaned up before morning. Sluggo's crew chief relayed to him another alert snow story. Keeping the alert Christmas Tree clear of snow was of course a major priority. In the fall months before the first snowfall, the plows and blowers would actually practice their removal routine in a "Conga Line." According to the crew chief, his partners in crime would hide a quart can of B-52 hydraulic fluid (which was a very bright red) in the snow in an area that they knew the snow blowers would cover. Yes, heart failure on the part of the plow driver when a giant blast of red snow came shooting out of his blower. On another snowy night, as the crew dogs were gathered in the rec room watching TV, one of the guys wanted to watch a different channel, he was voted down so he flipped to the channel he wanted, pulled the tuning knob off, (no remote available) opened the nearby door and threw the knob into the snow. Fearing a beat down, he pleaded it was only a moment of passion, begged forgiveness, and was booed out of the area. Channels were changed with pliers for the next few days.

Before we end this epistle, a couple more alert stories. Before leaving for the night, the chow hall dudes would put out some snacks for the troops. It was of the opinion that the quality and quantity of these goodies had decreased over time, so the crew dogs decided to cook their own snacks attacking the big refrigerators and cooking all manners of cuisine, being careful to clean up religiously before the mess crew showed up to cook breakfast. This went on for a while before the cooks got wise, wondering where all their food was going, and started locking the fridge's, not a problem for crew dogs who know where they kept the keys. After putting up with these antics for a while longer, the cooks said, "we'll show them" when the boys showed up the next time for a feast, to their chagrin the fridges were encased by large chains with padlocks…alas, no such thing as a free lunch anymore in the mole hole.

And perhaps, one of the greatest alert stories follows. The mole hole sleeping accommodations consisted of rooms with a sink and one or two beds…heads and showers down the hall. The usual configuration was two to a room: navigator (NAV) and radar nav (RN)…electronics warfare (EW) and co-pilot (CP), you get the idea. The pilot however, had a room by himself. As it turned out, because of the crew lineups there was usually one empty pilot room…which was up for grabs by anyone's use, first come first served. One of the EWs was obsessed with getting that room on every one of his alert tours. He would arrive at the mole hole in the middle of the night before alert changeover to ensure that he would get the solo room. It was reported that he would sleep in the hall outside the room with all his alert stuff and dash in as soon as the current occupant woke up on changeover morning. He would then crow (pun, EWs were nicknamed "Crows") at the turnover brief and in the chow hall, "well, I got the private room again; it will be a great alert tour." His EW and NAV brothers were growing sick of his boastful behavior, so they developed an elaborate plot to let him know what they thought about his deeds.

On the first night of alert, after he went to bed and when they were sure he was asleep, they crept down the hall to the closed door of his room and taped aeronautical charts (very large maps) to entirely cover the door frame on the outside (the doors opened in) top to bottom and side to side. Early the next morning they covertly assembled near his room to observe what would happen. A couple of tentative pushes on the paper, then a pencil poked through the charts followed by the EW tearing a hole in the paper and then a bigger hole, a look around, and finally yet a bigger hole and the EW exiting the room, stage left. The next morning the boys again covered his door with charts, again the reaction was much the same but with more bravado as the EW slowly burst through the paper. This was repeated the next day and the EW got ever bolder and literally did a superman takeoff through the papered door.

The next night the papering process was again repeated although slightly modified…a candy machine was moved in front of the papered door. You probably guessed it, the EW came charging through the charts, hitting the candy machine knocking it to the ground and scattering Milk Duds, Baby Ruth's, Junior Mints, and other confections throughout the hall. "Oh s…" echoed throughout the hallway. All the crew dogs involved got together and cleaned up the mess and the story that was told went like this; "it was an accident, one of the guys got up in the middle of the night to pee and stumbled into the candy machine knocking it over." The EW probably had a headache, other than that he was unharmed. He was a good egg about the whole thing and laughed as he rubbed his head, "you guys really got me good." The results; no harm, no foul, no retribution…and a great story. In spite of the frivolity discussed above, nuclear alert was very serious business and no one took it lightly, especially Sluggo and his mates, the SAC crew dogs.

Chapter Six: Hafa Adai and Welcome to Guam – "Where America's Day Begins"

As previously discussed, Sluggo departed the world on his first overseas deployment, "Operation Arc Light"... destination, a spot in the middle of the Pacific Ocean called Guam. The above maxim was, and still is written on a large sign on the Base Operations building at Andersen Air Force Base...Hafa Adai is "Hello" or "Goodbye" in Chamorro, like Aloha in Hawaiian. Over the next six years, Sluggo would have it up to there with both Arc Light and Guam.

There are many tales to be told about Guam, also known as the "Rock," Sluggo has selected only a few.

Guam is located in the western Pacific Ocean roughly half way between Hawaii and the Philippines...lots of water. Guam has been a U.S. territory since the Spanish-American War and is the largest island in the Marianas and Micronesia. 210 square miles of tropical paradise...no lie. It was occupied by the Japanese during WW II, no love lost there. Andersen AFB is tucked away on the North end of the island away from everything. Everything else including the Navy is located in the middle. Two roads lead from Andersen AFB to civilization. The Marianas Trench lies off the coast of Guam, 35,797 feet deep...who knows what lives down there...maybe the Kraken. Coral reefs surround the island, the North sports 500 foot cliffs, and the South is mountainous. Apra Harbor where the Navy lives is a deep water port, carriers, subs and other big boats. The economy of Guam is supported by two industries; tourism and the United States Armed Forces.

Andersen Air Force Base (AAFB), nee North and Northwest Field, Guam, was/is a major facility that was constructed during WW II, as the story goes, the Japanese started it and the Navy Seabees added on and finished it. The complex consisted of four runways, numerous taxiways and parking revetments for over 200 B-29 bomber aircraft, and associated facilities. The base mission was the bombing of the Japanese mainland (the atomic bombing missions were launched from Tinian Island 128 miles

North of Guam). B-29's also flew missions from AAFB during the Korean War. After the wars, the Northwest facilities were mothballed, and SAC adopted the remaining complex as a major Pacific base. As the story continues with the advent of jets, the runways were extended to over 10,000 ft. Since the coral  formations in the area were so difficult to level and construction was done in many phases, there is a significant dip in the middle of the runways where they were lengthened and added on. Lots of fun during takeoff and landings. BUFF pilots got so used to playing the dip on landing that when they returned to the real world of level runways...watch out for the first few landings...take that runway, and that, and that. At the end of the runway is a 500 ft. cliff down to the ocean. Good news for heavyweight takeoffs to the North, instant altitude; but landing in that direction was like landing on an aircraft carrier especially in a crosswind...great optical illusion that you think you're going to crash into the cliff and ergo you end up landing hot and long. It's reported that the waters off the end of the runway are littered with the remains of many a crashed aircraft including a few BUFFs.

The "Arc Light," the B-52 bombing campaign in Southeast Asia was "ignited" on Guam in 1965 with 27 B-52 F  model aircraft from CONUS bases participating in the first mission. It didn't go well; two BUFFs were involved in a midair collision resulting in the loss of both aircraft. The actual bombing was judged less than effective, but the bombs did hit the ground. Since the SAC planners were well versed in the nuclear mission, the process of refining the tactics, techniques, and procedures of a conventional bombing operation was a new problem that needed to be learned. In preparation for what was expected to be a long conflict, the B-52 D model (the most prolific made at 170) was significantly upgraded to perform the conventional bombing mission with major modifications to

the bomb bay and defensive equipment...it soon replaced the F models on Guam. The mission was tough, over 12 hours with an air refueling on the way over.

After fits and starts, the Arc Light slowly evolved into a viable operation. As a big sign on Bomber Operations stated "Our Mission, Bombs On Target"...this motto was certainly not conceived by crew dogs who needed no reminder what their mission was. Occasionally, the sign would

be defaced with crude comments inscribed on its surface. Would crew dogs be responsible for such antics...I wonder?

As discussed earlier, one night on Guam at the O Club, Irish became call sign "Sluggo." Andersen was also the scene of the crime of the stolen tug and Sluggo tree incident reported in a previous chapter. Living in the three story typhoon proof barracks in a compound, six to a suite was always sporty and led to some serious high jinx including a crew

dog falling off the second floor and breaking his neck, no Arc Light for him for a while...but he recovered. Another trick was building tennis ball cannons and shooting them at other barracks, some crew dogs went so far as to concoct homemade napalm as ammo. Motorcycle races around the barracks in the grass were also popular. One of Sluggo's best copilot friends, call sign Basie, one drunken night went back to the barracks (his crew was on the first floor) stripped off his clothes and jumped into bed and was soon in a booze induced coma. The gang picked him up mattress and all and deposited him in front of his squadron commander's door down the hall where he spent the night…quite an early morning surprise for his Lt Col boss.

The typical crew dog routine went as follows; check the flying schedule the day before, if flying load your gear on the AF blue bus three plus hours prior to takeoff and make your way to Bomber Operations, get the mission and intelligence briefs, check out your survival gear and weapon, try to grab a bite if you hadn't gotten one already, proceed to the flight line and your bird, get a maintenance brief, preflight the machine, start engines on the hack, taxi and get lined up for takeoff…you and two airplanes or you and five airplanes depending on the mission. Takeoff, climb out, and proceed a few hours later to air refueling, then coast in Vietnam, drop your bombs, and go feet wet for the flight back to the Rock and eat your inflight meal, greasy chicken anyone? Land, proceed to

mission, maintenance, and intelligence debriefings and you're done until the next time – but rest assured it will be sooner rather than later, all in a very long 20+ hour day's work.

The usual post flight procedure was to stop at Gilligan's Island outside of Bomber Ops. Gilligan's island was an outdoor patio with palm trees, multiple picnic tables and a roach coach, purveyor of snacks and cold beer open 24/7. In the early days of Arc Light, as per a tradition started in WW II, the post mission whiskey ration, a Flight Surgeon would show up at Gilligan's with bottles of Old Overholt Rye or Old Methuselah whiskey and two ounce dixie cups… without ice, the warm stuff was nasty and after a few tries business wasn't very good…eventually the Docs didn't show up anymore. A favorite crew dog meal was a chili dog heaped with onions. One morning when the boys showed up the cooks said, "no chili dogs today, we have chili but the wiener boat is late or has sunk." One enterprising guy asked if they had donuts and they said yes. "Well put some chili and onions on one"…and thus, a new Arc Light tradition, the onion chili donut was born.

One very sad day on Guam. Sluggo and crew had just flown an all-nighter and were in the rack getting some sleep when they were awakened by sirens and other noises. They went to the balcony to see what was going on. Some of the other guys said, "A BUFF has just crashed on takeoff; it was a crew from an Eastern base." Sluggo knew that his buddy Basie was scheduled to fly that morning. His worst fears were realized, observers stated that right after liftoff the left wing came off, the aircraft was fully loaded with fuel and bombs at the max gross weight, 450,000 lbs., the crew didn't have a chance to get out. Sometime later Basie's commander approached Sluggo "Since you were one of his best friends, would you call Basie's folks; they have already been notified of his death, I think it would mean a lot to them." He said, "you can come to the Command Post and we'll hook you up with a phone line." Sluggo said "of course I will, but I'll call them commercial on my own dime."

The only telephones capable of overseas calls were in the barracks laundry rooms, Sluggo made his way there and began the process of making an overseas call with his credit card. The room was stacked with mattresses so Sluggo settled in and waited for the overseas operator to call him back, after about a half hour he was connected with Basie's dad and they talked, at the end of the conversation his dad said "Basie brought a lot of light into every life he touched." Sluggo said, "Goodbye," hung up and then totally lost it sitting on the pile of mattresses. Years later, Sluggo visited the family several times and even went duck hunting with the dad. Every time Sluggo visits the Vietnam Wall he stops and gives Basie a high five.

What to do with your limited off time on Guam? There was always the outdoor movie theater, named the Washout, guaranteed to rain when a

good flick was playing. Tarague Beach was located in a large cove at the bottom of the cliff, fantastic snorkeling inside the reef, lots of colorful sea creatures, looking over the edge of the reef into the depths it

44

was coal black...for sure the Kraken lived down there, great snack bar with cold beer and edibles.

Bob Hope with Ann Margret and his show showed up for Christmas. When the first McDonalds opened on Guam it was declared an island holiday. There was also  a golf course, well known to Sluggo after his tug/tree incident, although tough to get a tee time. The Officers Club was quite palatial, huge dining area with stage, a 10 piece Philippine band with singers played most nights, classy (songs like *Leaving on a Jet Plane* and *We Gotta Get Out Of*  *This Place*, banned after several rowdy crew dog incidents), dress code, no green bags (flight suits) allowed, big fancy bar, package store, and stag bar (green bags allowed) where you could get a sandwich or something. Olympic sized pool and outdoor food and drink services. Needless to say there existed major angst between the temporary crew dogs and the permanent party stationed there.

During Linebacker II, the bombing of Hanoi, over 150 BUFFs and many crews were flying out of Guam and taking serious losses. Around Christmas, there was a stand down and crews at Andersen had a one-day respite. Guam based B-52s were shot down, many crew members lost. Crews went to the Officers Club for a good meal only to find out that the club was closed for an Officers Wives Club (OWC) function, the stag bar was open, but no food. This was not the right answer to many who had just lost friends and flying comrades. At the stag bar things rapidly got out of hand, and soon the Christmas decorations, trees and everything else from throughout the club ended up in the swimming pool, not a good scene but a mob mentality perpetrated by some angry individuals prevailed. Sluggo and most of the others watched but didn't participate or try to stop it, if they had, that probably would have caused a real brawl. The Air Police showed up but didn't intervene...smart... they let the event burn itself out, officers acting badly. Ugly show, but someone should have known given the situation, something like that might happen.

On a lighter note, looking at the map you can see that transportation was a major problem, lots of bus routes throughout the base, but real civilization was about 15 miles down the road. The solution, a "Guam Bomb." Guam Bomb was the endearing name given to crew dog cars. Many folks leaving the island for greener pastures would sell their cars instead of having them shipped back to the mainland. Crews would pool their money and buy one of the beaters, when their tours were up, they would recycle to incoming crews. To drive on base required no visible rust on bodies; lots of duct tape and spray paint fixed that. To go off base cars had to be registered with Gov Guam at the DMV in the capitol of Agana...quite an operation, nearly everything handwritten, and records really kept in shoe boxes.

Guam Bomb maintenance always a problem, lots of rust. One crew had a little rear engine auto that experienced complete motor failure on the back road to town...the engine fell out. Common condition of many, being able to see the ground through holes in the floorboards like a Flintstone car. Broken windshield wipers, no problem, run a string connected to the blades through the front windows, and the right seater manually controlled. One crew had a fuel pump go out, solution, hang a can of gas outside the passenger window and gravity feed. Cars too gone to save were sent to the auto graveyard and pushed over the cliff on the back side of the base...a good source of spare parts for future Guam Bomb repairs if you wanted to climb down and fight the spiders and other unknown creatures that lived in the wrecks.

The Sluggo crew first car was a 54 Chevy, good car but the radiator leaked and needed to be refilled on a regular basis when it heated up. One fine day the crew RN, call sign Macon, had a few too many beers at Tarague beach and forgot to fill the radiator from one of the many jugs of water kept in the trunk. The road from the beach was quite steep and with no cooling the engine gave up and froze after reaching the top...auto graveyard for the Chevy.

Another Sluggo crew car a few years later during Operation Bullet Shot was a 61 Pontiac, a great car lasted several tours. Towards the end of one tour the transmission started to go out, took it to the base gas station who did a great business with all the crew cars around, one speed forward, no speed backwards, said it couldn't be fixed, needed a new transmission. Checked around and there wasn't one on the island, went to the auto graveyard and searched, no luck. The crew was scheduled to rotate home in a week so they got the great idea we'll get a transmission at a junkyard when we're home and bring it back with us on our next rotation.

The EW, call sign Bird, who was a master wood worker, volunteered to make a box to carry the thing around on their redeployment. He constructed a beautiful wooden box complete with rope handles at each end. They bought a reconditioned transmission, wrapped it in plastic, put it in the box, and nailed it shut. The question, "What will we say when someone asks what's in the box?" After much thought, they addressed the box to General Dreedle, 3rd Air Division, Andersen AFB, Guam, in big letters (think of an infamous *Catch 22* character). As they boarded the KC-135 for Guam the crew chief asked "What's in the box?" the reply, "something for General Dreedle on Guam"… "OK, no problem I'll strap it down with the rest of the cargo." The boys got back to Guam, fixed the machine, and drove it until they left for good when the Arc Light finally went out; they ditched the car with the keys in it on Andersen AFB as a memorial to General Dreedle.

Anchors away my boys. The Navy occupied all the prime real estate on the island. Their exchange was the best. Their Officer's Club, the Top

of the Mar, was on the point atop the highest hill overlooking the harbor. Sluggo and the boys went there often. In the early days of the BUFF crew dog's occupation of Guam, the Navy club had parking spots marked "Reserved for Captains Only," since the boys were all Captains one guess where they parked. It didn't take long for the Navy to catch on and soon the signs read "Reserved for 06 Only."

One early evening the gang went to the Top of the Mar for their island famous Mongolian BBQ night. After a great meal and several drinks, they hooked up with some crew squids (naval version of crew dogs) from the Gold Crew of the USS Vallejo, a ballistic missile submarine that had just returned from nuclear patrol. They were accompanied by crew squids from the submarine tender USS Proteus, a semi-permanent fixture on

Guam where their boat was tied up. After lots of adult beverages and war stories, the Navy dudes invited the Air Force dudes to visit their boat…if they could in turn go see a BUFF. They said there is no time like the present, and the boys said, "Why not?" as they weren't flying for another day, so off they went to Polaris Point where the boats were parked. To make a long story short, they crawled all over the nuke U-boat until the sun came up and were then treated with a Navy  breakfast. The crew squids visited Andersen a few days later and watched a six ship B-52 launch up close and personal from the Charlie Tower. Sluggo thought the sub was much more exciting than the nasty old BUFFs, but he'd take the B-52 any day rather than plow underneath the ocean for many months at a stretch.

Naval Air Station Agana was the only other runway (built by the Japanese during WW II) on the island sharing space with commercial air (it's now A.B. Won Pat International Airport, sorry no more Navy). One cloudy day Sluggo's pilot and several other instructor pilots (three instructor pilots aviating together can spell trouble) were flying a proficiency sortie complete with touch and go landings at Andersen when a freak thunderstorm…out of the blue so to speak…hit the base. Visibility was quickly reduced to zero with violent wind gusts. They headed South with their BUFF hoping the storm would soon pass. Well, it didn't and perhaps got worse. About this time, the boys were getting very short on gas and with no improvement in sight, the decision was made to land at NAS Agana where the conditions were much better, but the runway was shorter and narrower, not especially BUFF friendly, in fact no one could remember a B-52 landing there. The approach was normal but at touchdown the aircraft suddenly veered to the right. There was a large wooden sign next to the runway that said WHEELS, a reminder to naval aviators to put their gear down. The pilots corrected and stayed on the runway but the outrigger landing gear (wheel), on the end of the wing plowed right through the WHEELS sign, no damage to the BUFF but the sign didn't make it. In retrospect, they determined that the crosswind crab, a capability to turn the quadracycle landing gear 20 degrees in either direction to enable the aircraft to takeoff or land in strong crosswinds was set in error. Well, the crosswind crab was set for landing at Andersen and the wind direction at Agana was in the opposite direction, oops. Egg on their faces and mud all over the side of the aircraft, and alas the poor sign.

That evening Sluggo's pilot sheepishly approached him and said "We need your help in the morning to make a cartridge start (discussed in a previous chapter, a copilot responsibility) on the BUFF at Agana cause there isn't any B-52 ground support equipment…we know how but haven't made one in years and we can't afford to screw this up. We'll fly the bird back; we just need you to fire the cartridges." A grinning Sluggo said "yes sir" and thought to himself "you'll owe me big time for this one." In the morning, they went to Agana and Sluggo made the cartridge start and the instructors flew the airplane and Sluggo drove the blue AF truck back to Andersen. Prior to takeoff, evidently the word had gotten out and the tarmac was lined with Navy dudes waiting to watch the show. The BUFF roared down the runway and broke ground in a cloud of smoke; blowing dirt and debris they received loud cheers from the swabbie crowd. The instructors landed and tried to low ball the incident, no harm no foul…and they got away with it…but they owed the Navy a new sign and Sluggo for his silence.

Sluggo flew his 100th and 400th combat mission from Guam and got the traditional post mission wet down…looks like he aged a bit after 300 more missions and four more years on the Rock.

There are many more Guam stories but since this Chapter is getting a bit long in the tooth…Hafa Adai and remember…Guam is Good!

Chapter Seven: Arc Light Two – "You're in the Army Now"

Back to nuclear alert and training. One day it was announced that to upgrade to instructor copilot (ICP) (no one really figured out just what the duties of an ICP were) Sluggo had to do another Arc Light tour with a new crew. So off again to school and back to Guam. Sluggo's new pilot was a jumpy sort, especially during air refueling... don't think he enjoyed flying within 20 feet at almost 300 knots behind another large airplane. One day closing in on the tanker, they stopped at the pre-contact position and the pilot said, "Take the aircraft." Sluggo stabilized as the pilot fumbled around in his seat. Sluggo glanced over and observed the pilot peeing in a coffee cup. After refueling the pilot explained he always got the nervous urge to pee before refueling and if he didn't have enough time to make it to the urinal, he did it in a coffee cup. As this tour progressed usually whenever it was night or in the weather Sluggo got the refueling duties...the pilot said it was good practice for him...Sluggo said, "Yes sir," and smiled to himself.

One dark night they were flying back to Guam after a combat mission as number three in a three-ship formation with one-mile separation between aircraft. It was Sluggo's turn to sleep, snuggled up in his ejection seat, and the pilot's turn to stay awake. The lead aircraft called a turn of about 15 degrees. Number one turned, number two turned, and Sluggo's pilot turned...they were on autopilot at the time. Half way through the turn the pilot fell asleep, the lead aircraft rolled out as did number two but good old number three kept right on turning, Sluggo finally nudged the pilot, he woke up and looked out the window to find the rest of the formation but they weren't where he expected them. He quickly turned back to rejoin, and you guessed it fell asleep again and kept on turning. Sluggo said, "Pilot, why don't you take a break...I'm wide awake." He said "OK, thanks, you've got the aircraft" and quickly went back to la la land.

One day after a mission debriefing some Strat Wing biggies approached the crew and said, "We need a B-52 crew to go in country with the Army to discuss BUFF operations and to show them that SAC crew dogs are real warriors." His pilot, (the guy that didn't like air refueling) said, "Well I don't know but I'll ask the crew." Sluggo thought, "What a great adventure and we'll get off the Rock for a while." He convinced the rest of the crew and so the trip was on, not sure the pilot was that excited...although it was good promotion stuff for him. In preparation for the trip they got several gloom and doom intelligence briefings including, "You should not advertise the fact that you're a B-52 crew, the bad guys have a price on your heads...wanted dead or alive...if captured your ass wouldn't even be grass. Your uniform will be flight suits, you must sanitize them, remove any unit patches especially patches that indicate you fly a B-52...only rank, wings, and name tags."

So off they went, they flew into Tan Son Nhut Air Base outside Saigon (not in a B-52...no stinking BUFFs on the ground in Vietnam...too big a target). They were met by some of the boys from MACV and 7th Air Force and their sponsors, Army II Corps Headquarters. After some glad handing and introductions, it was off in a bus to the infamous Rex Hotel. The II Corps guys said, "We'll met you for dinner at the hotel and pick you up early in the morning for some briefings then we'll depart for Pleiku Air Base up north in Kontum Province." After checking in at the Rex while riding the elevator up to their rooms, the young Vietnamese lad running the elevator commented, "Welcome to Saigon, you guys must be the B-52 crew." So much for the secret squirrel preparations to disguise their identity, they should have worn a sign "B-52 crew, have bombs will travel."

After dinner, they had some beers in the also famous Rex Rooftop Bar and watched the flashes from some air or artillery strikes far off in the distance. Sluggo soon repaired to his room for the night. At "0" dark thirty, he was awakened by someone pounding on the door, Sluggo jumped out bed and asked what "the hell is going on." The answer from the hall was "what are you doing in my room...open this door; I'm tired and need some sleep." He sounded American, so Sluggo opened the door and there stood a slightly disheveled Army captain complete with rucksack, helmet, and an M-16 rifle that he was leaning against. The guy said, "My key says room 225 and this is room 25." Sluggo said "This is room 25 alright, although this is room 325, you're on the wrong floor." The guy mumbled "Sorry, I guess I woke you up." Sluggo said, "No harm, no foul buddy, we captains must stick together." The guy staggered off and Sluggo went back to bed thinking "What's next?" Alas, no further action that night.

They were picked up in the morning, back to Ton Son Nhut for a battery of briefings. Their destination, Pleiku Air Base, was located in the central highlands near the tri-border area of Vietnam, Laos and Cambodia. The Cong and NVA regular bad guys were raising lots of hell in the area, Laos and Cambodia were major infiltration and supply routes into the South down the Ho Chi Minh trail, also Cambodia was a sanctuary...no bombing. The boys confirmed to their hosts that they had flown numerous BUFF strikes in the area against the trail. According to their Army tour guides, from Pleiku they were heading out to some of the more charming and rustic places in the area. Off the boys went to base operations where they boarded an Air Force C-7 Caribou. The Caribou was a medium sized two engine STOL trash hauler that the Air  Force stole from the Army several years earlier in a deal, "We'll take most of the fixed wings and you take most of the helicopters (except rescue)."

They were sharing the ride with about 15 ARVN Rangers and their U.S. advisors also headed to Pleiku. After takeoff Sluggo went up to the cockpit to check it out (remember from a previous chapter he had the choice of a Caribou out of pilot training...his pilot training roommate, call sign "Nogs" was flying them). "What a hoot it would have been if old Nogs was driving this baby," he thought, "nice little cockpit except why are the throttles on the ceiling?" Heading back to his seat...he didn't really have a seat, only webbing, he noticed some of the ARVN troops lighting a small fire in a container on the floor of the aircraft... fire on an aircraft...not good. He told the loadmaster about it and he said, "That's just normal procedure with those guys, they are just starting a barbeque to cook lunch, not to worry." "OK," said Sluggo, the rest of the flight was uneventful; the cooks even gave him a taste of some kind of mystery meat with a sauce that they had cooked, "not bad, but mighty, mighty hot."

The boys landed and were met and welcomed by an II Corps BGen, impressive, accompanied by the lucky guys that would babysit them for

the next few days. More area briefings and then over to the Air Force side of the base to meet the Air Commando, Special Ops blue suiters. They flew an odd collection of aircraft including A-1 "Skyraiders" left over from the Korean War, a mix of C-47 "Gooney Birds" left over from WWII in several configurations, psyop, leaflets and loud speakers "Bull Shit Bombers," ECM Birds and AC-47 "Spooky" gunships sporting three side firing 7.62 mm miniguns, also known as "Puff the Magic Dragon", and other

propeller driven flying marvels. The BS bomber guys told us the bad guys really liked the leaflet drops…free butt wipe. They invited them to come over to their hooch that night for a few beers. II Corps put the crew up in some old reconditioned former French Colonial quarters, quaint but nice; they expected a foreign legionnaire to pop out in any second. They ate some chow and made their way over to the special ops hooch's which were large, low slung buildings with blast walls, rooms, heads, and

showers…not bad. They reported that they had decided to declare war on the electronic countermeasure (ECM) squadron guys next door as they had just completed a screened-in outdoor porch and they didn't have one. Soon beer cans filled with water were flying through the air and slamming against both buildings including the new porch. An assembly line was set up in the showers to fill the beer cans and wash off the CS powder (tear gas ingredient) in bags that also flew through the air. After several frontal assaults with no winners, it was getting late so a cease fire was declared. "War is hell...and your friend may be your enemy," thought Sluggo as he limped back to his rack, (he was slightly wounded in action as he fell during one of the beer can and CS gas assaults.) Was alcohol a factor...I wonder?

At the crack of dawn, they made their way over to Dak To where they were given flak jackets and steel pots, the guys were already heavily armed with their Air Force stub nosed 38s...sure. As they waited around for a helicopter ride to the next garden spot, they noticed a big sign on the heliport that said, "No Loitering Due To Frequent Rocket Attacks." "Wonderful," thought Sluggo,  "then why the hell are we standing here?" Next stop, Ben Het Special Forces Camp.

Ben Het was a strategic asset located within spitting distance from Laos and Cambodia which meant that the bad guys were also within spitting distance from them. Lots of snooping and peeping and stuff went on at Ben Het and its environs. Ben Het was also the scene of the most  famous tank battle of the war. The gang was met by the camp heavies who said that the enemy had probed the defenses last night and were repulsed "come take a look, the 50 cals really chopped them up," with that two Cobra Gun Ships started to work out on the jungle area surrounding the camp. They were sitting around shooting the breeze on the open-air bunker on the high spot of the camp; Sluggo presented them with a bottle of good whiskey that he had smuggled in from Guam which they really appreciated. They presented the crew with several different AK-47 models.

While they were sitting there, several of the camp dogs started barking and hauling ass for cover, the guys yelled "we've got incoming" followed soon by rockets hitting the camp and a supply convey that was a few klicks away. Everybody went to ground. This went on for a while and the hosts said "this doesn't look good or normal; this doesn't usually happen during daylight, we'd better get you guys out of here ASAP or you might be here for a while, we'll see if we can get some Hueys in here PDQ." The choppers blew in during a lull in the action and low hovered to pick them up, the boys hauled ass aboard and they beat feet back to Dak To. As history would tell them, that was "day one" of the siege of Ben Het that went on for nearly two months.

The next day and the next event was a Chinook chopper ride to Fire  Support Base Six, an artillery stronghold on top of one of the highest hills (called "rocket ridge") in the area. On the chopper ride, Sluggo shot a few movies of the area. Fire Support Base (FBS) Six had some serious 155 howitzer firepower all resupplied by air because of the high terrain and the fact that the bad guys were very close, occupying most of the low surrounding areas around the FSB.

 One of the prime reasons the boys were there was to monitor a B-52 strike scheduled to go into the valley about three kilometers down the hill. It was not going to be a normal strike which was three BUFFs, in an offset bombing formation, but because of heavy enemy presence in the area, in this case it would be two cells of three aircraft each separated by a couple of minutes, if the bad guys thought they survived the first batch and came out of their holes hopefully the next cell would get them.

The Army provided a photographer to follow the boys around. In the picture, you can see the smoke rising from the first cell as the second cells bombs are going off, slightly offset from the first cell. Six BUFFs times  108 bombs equal 648 and a lot of grief falling down on Charlie. You can see the crew in the tin pots and flak jackets watching the show, you can't hear the cheers from ground pounders as numerous secondary explosions went off indicating there was some bad stuff down there that was now trash. And yes, the ground shook even up there. As the boys were getting ready to chopper out, a H-54 Sky Crane flew in to drop off some ammo and blew away everything that wasn't nailed down and some that was. Sluggo and company departed with lots of handshakes and good will and "keep the bombs coming."

Back to Pleiku, Saigon and back to Guam. The military rag, "The Stars and Stripes" did a 2-page article featuring the boys' trip. Although the event was exciting and a good ride, and hopefully boosted some troop morale, Sluggo decided he had made the right choice with the USAF and BUFFs. The Arc Light now shined with new meaning. 179 days went by and back home for Sluggo.

Chapter Eight: Hai Dozo – "Greetings From Kadena Air Base, Okinawa Japan"

As you may recall from previous chapters, when the "Arc Light" was burning bright the normal rotation of B-52 crews was Andersen AFB, Guam; U Tapao Royal Thai Navy Airfield, and Kadena Air Base, Okinawa. They would spend a month or so in each place then on to the next. There are many wonderful tales from Kadena, Sluggo will relate just a few. But first, a brief history lesson.

Okinawa is the largest of the Ryukyu chain of islands. It is roughly 400 miles south of Japan, 400 miles off the coast of China, and 300 miles north of Taiwan. The island has an area of 466 square miles and a population of 1.3 million. Back in the day, the Kingdom of  Ryukyu was independent of Japan with their own government, religion, language, and customs. In 1879, Japan annexed the entire Ryukyu archipelago. The monarchy was abolished and the King deposed. Hostility against Japan increased in the islands immediately after the  annexation in part because of the systematic attempt on the part of Japan to eliminate Ryukyuan customs; including the language, religion, and cultural practices...can you feel the love? Okinawa was the site of a long and bloody battle during World War II. During the 82-day-long siege, about 12,510 U.S. Army and Marine Corps troops, 95,000 Imperial Japanese Army troops, and 149,193 Okinawans, one quarter of the civilian population were killed...again no love for anything foreign or military.

After the war, the U.S. occupied Japan including the Ryukyuan Islands until 1952 when control was returned to Japan...but wait, not so fast, we'll keep Okinawa as it's a critical strategic location for the United States Armed Forces. The Japanese were OK with that because Okinawa isn't really Japan. The island hosts around 26,000 U.S. military personnel, Army, Air Force, and Marines about half of the total complement of the United States Forces Japan, spread among 32 bases and 48 training sites. U.S. bases occupy about 25% of the island's area. Any love there…what do you think?

Setting the stage; Kadena Air Base (KAB) was the gem of the Pacific for the USAF, it had the best of everything, and yes there were swimming

pools and yes there was a golf course, the Banyan Tree, fully qualifying it as official Air Force Base, and by the way, several long runways. When the air war in Vietnam was cranking up, the heavy breathers decided that there was an overwhelming need for lots of air refueling tankers in the region to gas up bombers out of Guam and fighter bombers flying out of Thailand and Vietnam and other aircraft in the area. Starting in 1964, the decision was made to deploy 110 SAC KC-135 Stratotankers to the theater, most were deployed to KAB and thus, Operation "Young Tiger" was born.

The KC-135 is the highly modified military version of the four-engine Boeing 707 (same engines as the old BUFFs but only half as many) with a

40 foot long flying refueling boom, (which means you have to fly about 30 feet hooked up and 300 mph to get any gas.) It entered service in 1957. Like the old B-52s it took water injection (note the black smoke) to get the fully loaded beast off the ground…hence the nickname "Water Wagon."

As with the B-52 moniker BUFF, Big Ugly Fat F…., the KC-135 was also known as the TIF, Tiny Insignificant F…. After major modifications and new engines – no water injection anymore – it's still flying today and will be for many more years. Sluggo's CONUS base had a tanker squadron that deployed on a regular basis to Kadena well before BUFFs ever got there. At home whenever they were around any BUFF crew dogs, they talked about what a horrible place it was with terrible facilities and we hate to go there. Although he kind of always doubted their stories, Sluggo soon found out that tanker toads were far from truthful.

One more factoid before the stories, by 1973, after nine years and two months of hard flying, the TIFs had flown a total of 911,364 hours and 194,687 sorties. They conducted 813,878 in-flight refueling and off-loaded more than eight billion pounds of fuel. Young Tiger was called the "First Tanker War" and Kadena was the private domain of the tankers toads…and don't you forget it.

In 1968, SAC deployed a small covey of BUFFs to KAB to increase the Arc Light operations tempo, the mission to Vietnam was much shorter and Guam and UT were being maxed out. But what will the Japanese and Okinawans think about bombing missions being flown from their turf, what do you think? Several months later, Japan

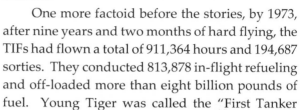

gave tacit approval to the U.S. to withhold from local residents the fact that the U.S. military was flying B-52 bombing missions in Vietnam from a base in Okinawa. It wasn't too tough for the locals to see the BUFFs with bombs hanging on their wings departing and coming back

eight hours later with no bombs…again no love there.

Copilot Sluggo departed Guam for KAB flying a D model B-52 a few months after the BUFFs first deployed there. It was his first trip to Okinawa better known as the "Big BX," more on that later. On the trip over they flew over Iwo Jima island, Sluggo thought "hard to believe that so many died on this little turd in the ocean." Well guess what, everything that the tanker toads said about Okinawa was a bald-face lie, after UT and Guam it was like going back to the real world. The BOQs were like posh hotels, two to a room except for the pilot who had a private mini suite, television, telephone, and house girls who for a small fee would do your laundry and even shine your flying boots…put your clothes in a bag and your boots outside your door…magic. The boys were also greeted with signs occasionally posted on BOQ bulletin boards stating, "BUFFs Go Home" and other nastier remarks…could the tanker toads be responsible…I wonder?

The O Club was amazing; huge, formal dining and fancy bar, bands at night (not really crew dog friendly), big snack bar (same food as fancy place), giant stag bar and yes, slot machines (all the clubs throughout the island had slots). The stag bar at the O Club was an all day and night operation. The bar looked to be about 60 feet long, behind the bar was a huge fish tank that went the length of the bar all the way up to the ceiling with all manner of aquatic flora and fauna creature; it separated the booze bar from the snack bar where families could eat their burgers and also watch the fish. The crew dogs got the  mandatory orientation briefings, local airdrome procedures, serious tensions exist with some of the locals…they really don't like us…and don't advertise the fact that you're flying combat missions from their island, and oh by the way there lives a snake here called a Habu…also known as tree viper…"They are large, venomous and can be aggressive when provoked, petting snakes is not a good idea."

The town outside the Kadena Main Gate was Koza City (now Okinawa City) and the Koza main drag was BC Street. BC Street was lined with shops of all descriptions, bars, massage parlors, trinket shops, restaurants, taxis to take you anyplace you wanted to go, and open air markets which were great once you got used to the smells, buy a bag of fried shrimp and a cold Kirin beer…great. Tailor shops proliferated.

Speaking of Habus; one morning after flying a night mission Sluggo and his buddy, the NAV, call sign "Ponse" were walking over to the O Club for some breakfast when they saw a group of house girls pointing to a tree and you guessed it, there was a snake hissing at them. Ponse declared "I think he's just waiting for a sweet, juicy copilot to come along." Sluggo said "not funny" as he had no love for snakes. The Habu exterminators came by and put the critter out of his misery. An occasional event in Koza was the infamous Habu Mongoose fight, the lightning quick mongoose usually won by faking the snake out and striking fast. There was also a liquor called "Habu Sake" alleged to have medicinal properties. The snakes were included in the fermentation process and it was sold in bottles that may contain the body of a snake…"to hell with snake guts, I'll stick to beer" thought Sluggo.

The SR-71 spy planes were also flying out of Kadena at that time…going who knows where, "I can't tell you or I'll have to kill you." They soon picked up the nickname "Habu" which stuck, the nickname "Mongoose" probably would have more

accurate due to their speed but who wants to be called mongoose. The SR-71 was an awesome machine, Sluggo and the boys got to be friends with several Habu crews, they were of course, royalty. They had their own BOQ building complete with the "secret bar," their own Flight Surgeon and ambulance…did the ambulance ever go downtown on

special missions…I wonder? One SR crew on their last mission buzzed the O Club pool "most impressive" thought Sluggo. The SR-71 motto displayed proudly on their ops wall was "Though I Fly Through the Valley of Death I Shall Fear No Evil - For I am at 80,000 Feet and Climbing".

One of the crazier BUFF crews came up with idea to take a Habu flying on their missions. They carried around a snake basket affixed with a lock and claimed there was a Habu inside. Mission briefings, preflight, flight, debriefings, the basket never left their sight. Through the slight slits in the basket you could see that there was something in it. They claimed that they kept in a refrigerator and fed it when it went into hibernation…they named the snake Irving. Irving ended up flying 33 combat missions and they talked about putting him in for an Air Medal. Unbeknownst to anyone else the colonels, worried about a poisonous snake flying Arc Light missions, called the crew in to get the real story and they boys admitted that Irving was rubber...the colonels agreed to keep the secret...and another legend in crew dog lore was perpetuated. "Did you hear about the BUFF crew that flew around with a pet snake?"

All was not peace and light in Okinawa. Over the years of U.S. occupation and military presence on the island, numerous serious incidents including murder, rape, hit and runs, road incidents, burglary, and general mayhem at the hands of U.S. servicemen stirred the pot of discontent with the American military.  Many GIs involved in these incidents were acquitted at courts martial. These incidents fueled the growing dissatisfaction of Okinawans with what they felt were unfair court decisions and the standard status of

 forces agreement that exempted U.S. servicemen from Okinawan justice. By 1970, it had already been decided and was widely known that the U.S. military occupation of Okinawa was going to be ended in 1972, and that Okinawa would return to being a part of independent Japan, but alas, a very considerable U.S. military presence was to remain.

Adding to the problems there were many accidents involving military vehicles and equipment—some resulting in the death of civilians. At Kadena, a KC-135 crashed on takeoff near a highway killing all on board and a civilian motorist. An SR-71 crashed on landing. A B-52 fully loaded on an Arc Light mission crashed on takeoff, went off the runway and hit a culvert – two crew were killed  five injured. The aircraft was totally destroyed and some bombs cooked off during the fire shaking the neighborhood.

There were many demonstrations near the base especially during BUFF launches. On a night in 1970 on the main drag in Koza City, a drunk

American Service member driving his car hit an Okinawan man who was helped into an ambulance with minor injuries. A swarm of pissed off onlookers started gathering, the angry mob began harassing uninvolved American Service members in the area. The Sky Cops showed up and what followed is known as the "Koza Riot" a violent and spontaneous protest against the U.S. military presence in Okinawa.

During that night and into the next morning of the following day around 5,000 Okinawans clashed with roughly 700 American military police in an event which has been regarded as symbolic of the Okinawan anger against 25 years of U.S. military occupation. In the riot, approximately 60 Americans

were injured, 80 cars were burned, and several small buildings on Kadena near the main gate were destroyed or heavily damaged…can you feel the love now? Before you ask, Sluggo wasn't there, he was flying out of Guam.

On a lighter note, Okinawa was truly the land of the "Big BX," or base exchange, or USMC exchange, or post exchange or whatever you want to call them. Lots of goodies and being so close to Japan wonderful prices and the U.S. dollar was the currency of the day both on and off base, another thing the natives weren't happy with. Sansui tuners, amps, and giant speakers, Teac reel to reel tape decks, Sony everything, Pentex and Nikon cameras and every lens known to man…and the list goes on…load it all on a TIF, fly it to Guam and then home and then neighborhood beware, sonic boom coming.

Copilot Sluggo was back to Kadena with the pilot that didn't like refueling (remember him from a previous Chronicle) bragging about his wonderful private suite complete with a large tiled bathtub. As it was close to July 4th, the boys procured some associated pyrotechnics and detonated a rather large string of firecrackers near the door of the pilot as he was taking a bath. As the crackers were going off an earthquake hit the area (Okinawa being in the Pacific "ring of fire" was prone to frequent quakes). The guys pounded on the pilot's door and he came running out wrapped in a towel yelling "that wasn't funny – what kind of fireworks did you guys buy that made the water in my bathtub splash?" The answer from his faithful crew was, "Put some clothes on and get out, it's an earthquake." There was only minor damage to the base. A couple of weeks later the boys gathered in the pilot's suite and watched on a black and white TV as the first NASA astronauts landed on the moon…narrated in Japanese.

A few more tales of Okinawa. The Kadena stag bar was melting pot of Air Force and other aviators; BUFFs, TIFs, fighters, bombers, recce, air lifters, rescue, special ops, you get the idea, mostly peaceful but at times tensions were sometimes flying through the air …could alcohol be a factor, I wonder? Back in the corner was a world famous 24/7 poker game, players came and went and at times big money was on the table. One night after flying that day, the crew NAV, Ponse stopped by Sluggo's place and said, "Come down to my room, you've got to see this." Ponse was sharing a room with the crew RN, call sign "Macon." There was Macon clad only in his shorts laying on top of his bed in a stupor with his mouth wide open, snoring loudly with drool seeping down his chin, covered with money of many denominations. Ponse said, "A few minutes ago he came staggering into the room saying "I finally beat those bastards," peeled off his clothes, flopped down on the bed, started throwing money up in the air and promptly passed out, I guess he finally won at poker." Sluggo thought, "Sleep tight Macon you'll feel like hell in the morning."

Copilot Sluggo returned to KAB again with "Gay and Beth the Killer Team" (named in a following chapter.) After they landed they made it over to the BOQ office where they were told there was no room in the inn and they would be staying in the "flattops" for a week or more. The flattops were single story barracks-like quarters, four beds and a sink to a room, toilets and showers down the hall….the boys weren't happy after Thailand, looking forward to the palatial BOQ. Sluggo and his pilot Beth were sharing one of the rooms with four beds. Off they went to the O'Club eatery and bar for a night of it as they were in orientation the next day and weren't flying. At the bar, they met one of Beth's old friends, a stew from one of the contract airlines that hauled GIs back and forth across the pond. Sluggo had also met her a couple of times before and thought, "She's a good one." She was well on her way to a horror show as she wasn't flying either for a couple of days.

To make a long story short, she was in no shape to go back to her off base hotel and the guys were in no shape to take her there. The boys thought, "We have two extra beds; she can crash in the flattops." And so, she did, out like a light. In the morning she awakened wondering where she was and needing desperately to use the bathroom. Sluggo thought, "There's bound to be guys shaving and showering down the hall, we need to run interference" which they did to the surprise of the troops. She used the facilities wrapped in a sheet so no one would see her stew uniform and got a taxi back to her hotel. Later that morning, during orientation Beth got a call from the BOQ office informing them that they would be moving from the flattops to the palatial BOQs post-haste and not in two weeks...I wonder why?

One of the crew dogs' favorite haunts were the tailor shops on BC Street in Koza. They did outstanding work and the price was right. Besides dress suits, one of the mandatory purchases was a "party suit" tailored flight suit like garment, wild colors, patches and embroidered doodads strictly for non-flying functions. Sluggo decided to have a special Saint Patrick's Day suit made, he selected a bright kelly-green material with small purple pinstripes. When he brought the material to the tailor the guy said, "No, no suit – drape or curtain only." When Sluggo asked, "But can you make a suit out of this?" the answer was "Yes." A couple of weeks later Sluggo picked up a glorious green double-breasted suit complete with covered buttons.

The boys decided to have crew pants made; they selected a pale blue material with large pink hibiscus blossoms. The tailors must have thought that flying long hours have certainly affected these guy's brains, but they've got money and so be it. After picking up their crew pants, the boys decided to debut their outfits at the stag bar since they weren't flying the next day. The crew pants were a mixed blessing some loved it and some didn't. There were lots of socially incorrect sexual references to the pants wearers and Beth almost came to blows...but he was much bigger and it didn't happen.

An F-105 "Thud" fighter squadron was celebrating their return from flying missions in Vietnam so the place was over wild. According to crew dog lore, one of the old heads bet one of the young captains that he couldn't swim the length of the bar fish tank (remember the fish tank). There was a ladder to the top of the tank on the far end of the bar and a catwalk above the ceiling for maintenance and cleaning. Well you guessed it, in he went with fish hauling ass and plants and water splashing everywhere. He didn't get far before the staff and his buddies pulled him out. Imagine the people, including some families eating at the snack bar on the other side of the tank…think an unexpected aquatic show worthy of Sea World.

The big brains got together and decided in light of the riot and near continuous protests, to end the BUFF combat missions from Kadena. So, in 1970 after 30 months of flying, the Arc Light went out in Okinawa, never to be rekindled.

To this day, U.S. military presence on Okinawa remains a serious issue.

Chapter Nine: Arc Light Three – "You're in the Army Again"

It was time for Sluggo to checkout as aircraft commander which he did in record time. But wait…not so fast ace. Capt Sluggo was informed he would have to go Arc Lighting again as a copilot prior to getting his own crew…the old carrot and stick routine. Sluggo was paired with one of the most notorious and crazy "Select" crews in SAC…Sluggo was right at home. The pilot's middle name was Macbeth and the radar navigator's (bombardier) first name was Gaylord, so they were better known as *Gay and Beth the Killer Team*. The crew was always in some kind of hot water, but due to their experience (the first B-52 crew in SAC to fly 1,200 combat missions) they usually got away with it.

Sluggo and "Gay and Beth the Killer Team" were flying out of U Tapao Royal Thai Navy Base commonly known as UT. The AF commanding one star was an old buddy of the pilot and met the crew one day after landing from a mission. He joined them for a beer and said, "I'm sending you guys in with the Army in Vietnam for a week…I'd do anything to get you crew bums out of my hair and off my base even sending you in with the ground pounders, and you Beth, you'll fit right in being a former West Pointer" …a big Ha Ha Ha went all around. A week or so later the guys departed UT for Bien Hoa Air Base, Vietnam in a C-47 "Gooney Bird" at about the same airspeed as a flat-out NASCAR stock car. They had to fly around the coast of Cambodia since Cambodia  was a strict no fly zone. Bien Hoa was a big AF base with lots of different stuff going on, it was about 16 miles from Saigon parallel to the "Parrots Beak," the outcropping of Cambodia land that poked into Vietnam (that should have tipped the boys off but didn't). Chow and beers at the O Club, then sleep.

The next morning, they got the mandatory battery of Air Force and Army briefings and met their Army hosts who told them, "Guess what guys, in the morning we're all going to Cambodia and we don't mean Angkor Wat." "Here's some flak jackets and tin pots, and we can see that you're already heavily armed with your USAF stub nosed 38s." For the record, a large combined U.S. and ARVN force had entered Cambodia for the first time on the ground a couple of weeks earlier after a lot of political what ifs at the highest levels. The ARVN and  Special Ops had done some sneaking and peeping before, but this was the big one...out in the open for all to see. The bad guys had been amassing vast stockpiles of weapons, ammo, equipment, and supplies for a long time via the Ho Chi Minh trail. They thought, "Because this is Cambodia, not to worry, the enemy can't touch us"...wrong this time. The crew would be flying in via four or five Huey's on resupply sorties to FSB Myron and FSB Bronco well into Cambodia.

As they were waiting to board their bird, the crew EW, call sign "RJ" said, "I can't go right now, I think I have the Ho Chi Min's revenge and must find a head ASAP." Sluggo said, "I'll wait with you; we can catch the next bird that's due in about 10 minutes." The helo crew said, "We're  leaving, hop the next flight" and they took off. RJ found a head and emerged about 10 minutes later looking rather pale but OK and they caught the next flight out. They found out later that the first Huey that they should have been on had a major rotor malfunction and had to make an emergency landing. Sluggo thought, "If RJ has the urge to go, that's an omen and his wishes are my commands."

As they were climbing on the next bird, the pilot said, "Captain have you ever flown a helo?" As Sluggo hadn't, the pilot said, "After we get leveled off, jump in the left seat and we'll see how you do" (in a helicopter the pilot flies from the right seat and the copilot in the left, as opposed to a fixed wing machine where the pilot flies in the left and copilot in the right). "Can do," Sluggo said. He got in the seat and started to fly, some turns, some slight climbs and descents, piece of cake, feels good. The pilot said let's try playing with the collective lever. "Why not?" said Sluggo, not really knowing what it did, followed then by a big "oops, that's different, think I need to practice that up and down stuff…don't think I'll be a rotor head any time soon."

While winging their way into Cambodia, the Army guys with them said, "Look at those bomb craters, they look like a B-52 strike went in a long time ago, they're filled with water." RJ said, "That was us, and we've been bombing Cambodia for a while." "Operation Menu" was the covert and classified B-52 bombing of select areas of Cambodia that went on well prior to the ground action. It was directed and approved at the highest levels in Washington including POTUS himself and only briefed to a few heavies.

The missions were directed from the ground by "Combat Sky Spot" using an elaborate mix of MSQ radar, computers, and air/ground communications. USAF MSQ sites were in Vietnam, Laos and Thailand usually on the tops of high hills, and usually not in nice neighborhoods. They had call signs like Milky, Bongo, Macon, Lima and others. Sluggo had been talking with them for so long (BUFF copilots did most of the communicating with MSQs) that some of the controllers would recognize his voice, and say, "Hi Sluggo, you still here?"

Combat Sky Spots directed the bomb runs of fighter and bombers at night and in any weather conditions within an accuracy of around 11 yards (not bad with 60's technologies). In extreme cases, they directed close air support of ground troops right up to the wire in siege areas like the Marines at Khe Sahn (Sluggo dropped a lot of iron there). The procedure for bombing in Cambodia was for the BUFF cell to contact the MSQ site, give them a code word, change to a discrete frequency, follow their direction to the target, (only the lead aircraft would be guided, the other two aircraft would fly a loose formation on lead and compute the time and distance for release) drop the weapons and exit repeating the code word and going about their flight home.

The guys landed in Cambodia without incident, met the troops, got briefed, and watched an artillery battery do its thing (Sluggo was always attracted to cannon fire following his college years). As the story goes, one of the village chieftains had come up to the FSB perimeter and stated, "You're welcome here, but could you direct your fire in a different direction as it's going directly over by my village and disturbing my people and livestock."

After chow and more mingling with the troops, the guys hit the rack, but not Serta's, in various hooches. Sluggo had met a fellow captain and he invited him to stay at his pad as his roommate was away in Saigon. Sluggo was sound asleep dreaming of sugar plum fairies or something, when all hell broke loose, explosions going off everywhere. "Shit, the place is under attack," thought Sluggo. His roommate, the Army captain was laughing his butt off; Sluggo asked, "What's so damn funny?" "I forgot to tell you about mad minutes" was the reply. "What the hell are mad minutes," asked Sluggo. "Mad minutes are a drill when everyone on the perimeter fires all their weapons out into the jungle for a minute, the times are random every night so the gomers don't ever know when it's coming, supposed to keep them from sneaking up on us" he replied. "I'll bet you forgot to tell me you ass...let's watch the Air Force guy do the funky chicken" thought Sluggo. Army said, "Let's go outside and check it out," so they went out to the berm, fired a bunch of rounds from M-79 grenade launcher into the air and went back to their racks.

The next morning, they choppered into another firebase, on the way Sluggo noticed a big round clearing in the middle of the jungle. "What's that" he asked. The Army LTC with them said "that's from a "daisy cutter" bomb that they drop out of a C-130." The Air Force program was called "Commando Vault," the bomb was a BLU-82, 15,000 lbs. of love, designed to go off seven feet above the ground to create an instant landing zone or golf hole, or waterpark, or whatever. The bomb was so big that even a BUFF couldn't carry one, so delivery was rolling it out of the back cargo ramp of a C-130. A few weeks earlier, Sluggo was flying at altitude on a mission over Cambodia and saw one go off on the ground, looked like a nuke, impressive.

After meeting and greeting the troops at the firebase, they had some chow and the Army LTC said "I've got a patrol out working in the area, let's go give them a visit" so off they went in a Huey. After a few minutes of flying they started to circle, "We're directly above them, I told them to pop smoke and we'll see if we can land." Sluggo looked out and saw a little slit in the jungle with smoke billowing out, "That hole looks mighty small to me," he thought. In they went, mowing a few branches down with the rotors on the way, they landed on a pile of logs and got out and met the troops who said that there were some bad guys a few klicks away. After talking with the troops for about an hour, the LTC said it was time to leave. However, the chopper pilot informed him that he didn't have enough power to get out with all the passengers on board...some will have to stay behind.

You guessed it, since Sluggo was the lowest ranking of the bunch he and the LTC would stay behind. The others left; the pilot said he would be back as soon as he could. While they were waiting, a few mortar rounds hit the jungle near them, "that's not good" thought Sluggo. After about an hour the Huey was back, they popped more smoke and down he came, picked them up and off they went back to the firebase. The LTC told Sluggo, "If you need a job, I can always use a sharp Company Commander, you're cool under fire." Sluggo thought, "Thanks for asking but no thanks, and why have all the places I visited tend to come under attack?" They left Cambodia, next stop, Bien Hoa Air Base.

The next morning, they hopped on their trusty Gooney Bird to fly back to U Tapao and their beloved BUFFs. They were the only passengers on the plane. However, lining the walls of the aircraft and strapped down was a large herd of the big white and green ceramic elephants that

 Vietnam was noted for. The pilots came back before takeoff and said, "These beasts are destined for the Officers Wives Club Store in Okinawa, if we run into any engine  problems or any other glitches on the way back; your mission is to throw those babies out of the hatch." All went well, and both the boys and the elephants landed safely in Thailand; back to the land of the BUFF.

Once again, a Sluggo lesson learned; "I would rather fly than pound the ground, I think I'll continue to let the Arc Light guide my way," he mused. Another 179 days and homeward bound.

Chapter Ten: Sawadee Krap – "Greetings from U Tapao Royal Thai Navy Airfield"

As you may recall from previous chapters, when the "Arc Light" was burning bright the normal rotation of B-52 crews was Andersen AFB, Guam; Kadena Air Base, Okinawa; and U Tapao RTNA, Thailand; better known as UT. They would spend a month or so in each place then on to the next. There are many wonderful tales from UT, Sluggo will relate just a few. But first, a small history lesson.

Bilateral relations between the Kingdom of Thailand and the United States date back to 1818. Ever since then, Thailand and the U.S. have been  close allies and partners… it was the first Asian nation to have a formal diplomatic agreement with the United States…who would have guessed that. Thailand was a defense member of the now defunct SEATO and the still active Manila Pact; they were also designated a "major non-NATO ally." Thailand was a voluntary and active participant in the Vietnam War including deploying troops to South Vietnam to protect its own borders as well as helping to bring stability to the region as a whole. Thailand provided air and ground bases to the U.S. from 1961 to 1975; the USAF installed seven air bases in the country. These bases held more than 400 aircraft and 25,000 GIs. More than 80% of the airstrikes during the war were carried out from Thai bases. The U.S. also expanded the country's infrastructure with modernizing highways from the upgraded deep water port of Sattahip (next door to U Tapao) to the Northern air bases. In 1965, USAF KC-135 tankers were flying refueling missions  from Dong Muang airport outside Bangkok. The visibility of large USAF aircraft flying combat missions from the nation's capital was causing political embarrassment for the Thai government. The decision was made to hide the tankers at the small Thai Navy Airfield, U Tapao, some 90 miles south of Bangkok, but alas, major improvements were required to make that happen. The expansion of UT included building major facilities and a 11,500 foot runway, the work began in 1965 and it became operational in '67. The KC-135s were moved to UT...never to darken Bangkok's doorstep again.

The heavy breathers and big thinkers at SAC, 3rd Air Division, and

elsewhere mused, "Why don't we do a major expansion at UT and move a covey of BUFFs down there; the missions would be about four hours long with no air refueling necessary and we can greatly expand our sortie rate, after all, our goal is "bombs on target." The B-52 mission from Guam is over 12 hours long and needs air refueling, flying out of Okinawa is also a long haul and the natives want us to leave big time, the Philippines, Taiwan, and South Vietnam are non-starters for BUFFs, so let's do Thai." An agreement between the Thai and U.S. governments allowed 15 BUFFs and support personnel to be based at UT with the

provision that missions flown from Thailand would not fly over Laos or Cambodia on their way to their targets in Vietnam. In April 1967, three Guam based B-52 Ds dropped their bombs in Vietnam and recovered in UT. The

very next day BUFF combat operations began from U Tapao. Tankers and bombers, dogs and cats, living and working together in perfect harmony, why not?

Copilot Sluggo hit the ground at UT in 1967, what a place, a whirlwind of activity and construction and wow the humidity, dripping armpits in 20 seconds and an odor, not nasty or bad but strange and different...the aroma of Asia...he'd never forget it. Crews living in hooches and thrown together barracks, a primitive O Club/bar/restaurant…"But where's the golf course and swimming pool, all USAF bases have them?" "So sorry GI, no hab," but UT did have a beach…Sluggo loved the country immediately. Off to crew orientation: Thailand and UT rules, "No overflight of Cambodia, be prepared to fly almost every day you will get some breaks, trust us. If you have a serious emergency after takeoff, jettison your bombs in this designated offshore area." The flight surgeon imparted some words of wisdom, "Don't pet any snakes, most are two steppers, you get the idea." "Don't swim in a klong (Thai waterways) you might die…we don't know what critters live in there." "If you fall in love downtown, be advised you might be coming back to see me soon." And holding up a large jar of water, "This is from off base, see the particles floating around in there, well that's poop, don't drink it"…and holding up another jar, "This is on-base water, see the particles floating in here, well that's poop too, but it's clean poop, so go ahead and drink it."

The flying out of UT was great, takeoff, turn to the north (that's the big "N" in pilot talk), sneak across Laos (what overflight?) cross into Vietnam, drop your bombs, sneak back out and head home, cross into Thailand and turn to the big "S" (I'll bet you figured out that's pilot talk for south) let down, approach UT and land, taxi in, debrief and have a few beers…all in a respectable days work and do this five or six days a week.

Of course, one of the crew dog quests was who can fly the shortest combat mission? The old crew dogs soon figured out if you cut the corner around Cambodia you can slice a few minutes off the flight. So originally a few miles into Cambodia, then a few more and a few more then finally screw it, right across Cambodia…what's the threat from the Cambodian Air Force…none. Crews started getting back to UT earlier and earlier, in debriefing when asked how, "We had great tailwinds." The early arrivals started to screw up the subsequent launches as UT had only one runway. It didn't take long for the brass to figure out what was going on, so the word came down, "Tail winds my ass, we know you guys are flying over Cambodia so knock it off, now." BUFF folk lore claims that the record mission before the crackdown was slightly less than three hours. Copilot Sluggo flew on the first B-52 mission against the Plain of Jars in Laos. It was a night mission with 18 BUFFs in three ship cells. The target was a transshipment point on the Ho Chi Min trail where the NVA had stored countless tons of supplies, POL, munitions, rice, etc., out in the open on their way to South Vietnam. The aircraft alternated between iron bombs and CBU's (cluster bombs)...after release it looked like the 4th of July down there. When the war ended, the USAF and BUFFs had flown thousands of bombing sorties in

Laos...it was then and still now known as "The Secret War."

On a lighter note, what did the crew dogs do on their limited time off? The yet unspoiled Bangkok was a wonderful city with lots of great scenery, Sleeping and Emerald Buddha's, Pagodas, Floating Market (super back in the day), and more, Sluggo said, "Very cool stuff." Numerous jewelers were very happy to provide a van ride to their shop from UT with a guaranteed trip back. Sluggo and crew were partial to one called *Venus Jewelers*, commonly known to them as *Venus Cleaners* as they cleaned out your money, but their stuff was first rate and they were all good guys. Then there was Pattaya Beach just a few klicks up the road from UT. How to get there? In a Bhat Bus of course, (pick-up with seats in the back) waiting outside the base main gate (the Bhat was Thai currency worth a nickel then.) The fares depended on where you wanted to go, "one man one Bhat, one man five Bhat" you get the idea. Pattaya was a little known paradise, a quiet fishing village with one paved road around the bay, a couple of very small European run hotels and restaurants and bars on stilts over the water, great food and music, a peaceful place to really kick back. At one bistro you could order a giant caldron of mussels cooked in butter and white wine with a huge basket of fresh French bread...heaven.

You could also rent a fishing boat, captain, and mate for a few Bhat and throw in a bottle of Scotch or a carton of Salem Cigarettes (the King smoked Salem's) and you were good to go for all day including some snorkeling and a stop at the islands for a beach lunch. Sluggo and his copilot, the infamous "Big Dave" went fishing on a day off, several (many) beers were consumed. Big Dave hooked a fish and was reeling it in and the mate was about to net the catch. He turned pale when he saw it was a sea snake...very, very poisonous... remember the "two steppers" we talked about, well a sea snake was a "one stepper." So he cut the line and yelled, "Mi di!" which means very bad in Thai...no snorkeling there.

They stopped at an island for lunch, beached the boat and ate the fish they caught over a charcoal grill accompanied by the Thai traditional rice dish purchased from a beach stall, khaw phad, fried rice with an egg on top, better known to crew dogs as "cow pot." The boat crew was dining on a clear soup with some little green things floating around. Big Dave who was quickly going native, said he'd like to try some of that. The crew said, "No, no very hot." Big Dave said, "I'm from Texas and I like hot food. " The crew said "OK" and Big Dave took several mighty swigs. In about 30 seconds Big Dave let out a blood curdling scream and ran into the ocean shoveling sea water into his mouth...real Thai food is very, very hot...did he learn a lesson? I think not. Pattaya Beach, Paradise Lost...sad. Several thousand residents then; 500,000 inhabitants now and in peak tourist season 1,000,000.

Back to flying—by now there were over 50 BUFFs operating out of UT. On one mission as they were approaching the base, Big Dave thought one of the gas tanks wasn't feeding properly. Sluggo said "let me see your fuel log." The copilot owned the mysterious BUFF fuel panel with a myriad of switches and tanks. Big Dave passed his clipboard to Sluggo and in doing so it slipped out of his hand and smote Sluggo a mighty blow to the nose including a splash of blood. Sluggo yelled over to Big Dave... "Let's stage a fight so the rest of the crew thinks we're going at it". So lots of swearing from both over intercom, "I'm bleeding you dumb ass," and more. The rest of the crew was worried and expressed their concern over intercom, "Is everything all right up there?" As they about to land the EW came to investigate, Sluggo and Big Dave started laughing and the crew relaxed. "Good landing Big Dave, let's go get a beer."

A few words about bombs, the D model Buff could carry 108, 84 in the bomb bay, 24 on the wings, lots of iron. In case of a serious emergency after takeoff, the BUFF would be too heavy to land with the bombs onboard. The procedure was to proceed to a jettison area about a mile off the beach and drop the bombs in safe mode in the water, no problem. But wait, in some high-sea situations, the bombs were being swept onto the shore. During one patrol off the beach, the Sky Cops encountered a couple of Thai lads trying to cut open a 500 pounder with hacksaws to get the explosive out to be used for fishing (like the DuPont Spinner known to some American anglers). So the solution was to jettison the bombs armed, lots of boom but they wouldn't show up on the beach anymore. Not so fast GI, the Thai fishermen (soon to be targets) would see a BUFF circling off the beach and haul ass in their boats to the area awaiting the hordes of fish that would float to the surface after the bomb bursts...damned if you do, damned if you don't.

Occasionally, for whatever reason, a bomb wouldn't release properly...a hung bomb, called a "hanger" usually wasn't really a big problem. The BUFF RN (bomb aimer) owned the weapons, an indicator light on his panel would go out when the bomb released...bombs away...lights out. One of Sluggo's pilot buddies had a hanger on the wing rack and as he landed at UT the bomb released at touchdown. He said, "I looked out the window and the bomb was bouncing along beside us down the runway...we finally left it in the dirt...it didn't go off."

On one mission Sluggo's RN, call sign Mack, informed him that they had a hanger in the bomb bay, and one light was on. They informed ground before landing and were directed to the hot pad after landing where munitions maintenance (MMS) would pin (safe) the bomb. The MMS crew was waiting for them and evidently their ground intercom wasn't working, and they signaled Sluggo with gestures to enter the bomb bay and got a thumbs up. A couple of minutes later, they popped into Sluggo's view signaling cut engines and haul ass, Mack informed the crew that his light had gone out, the bomb had dropped and it was time to get the hell out of dodge. Sluggo informed the tower that they were shutting down and, "This airplane doesn't belong to us anymore, it's all yours, send a crew bus." The bomb had indeed released but the MMS guys managed to get a chain around it and it didn't fall far, no harm, no foul, no boom.

One more bomb story. The last bomb to be released typically was a leaflet bomb commonly known as a Bull Shit Bomb. It stated "Your day

 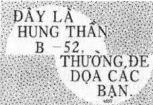

ĐÂY LÀ
HUNG THẦN
B-52.
THƯỜNG ĐỂ
DỌA CÁC
BẠN.

was just ruined by a B-52, go home and it won't

happen again," or words to that effect. Reliable sources on the ground confirmed the leaflets were highly prized by the bad guys who used them as butt wipe. More than half a billion leaflets were dropped by the USAF during the war, a major slice by BUFFs.

Back on the ground for a few last tales. As reported in previous chapters, in the glory days of UT, the crews lived in prefab pads known as "the trailers" 50 or more in a field with roads crisscrossing the area. All the staff big boys lived in a row of trailers at the far end. At the other end was the new and improved O Club. You could really screw with your buddies by unplugging their trailer's electricity and turning off the water, they were all module don't you know, did that ever happen?...I wonder.

It was an unwritten crew dog rule that vehicles with the keys left in were fair game for grand theft auto. One night after a few beers at the O'Club, the boys spotted a beat-up jeep parked with top down and keys in. So a few guys jumped in and drove it back to the trailer park and left it next to the trailer of a crew that they knew was on break hoping they would get the blame. A day went by and the jeep was still there, then another day, then a week...still there. The boys thought it's a trap, the OSI probably has it staked out and if anyone approaches, they will be nabbed. Finally, the boys couldn't take it anymore, after an early evening landing the blue crew bus dropped them and two other crews off at their trailers near the jeep. The other crews had heard of the jeep mystery. Sluggo's guys said, "Screw it let's drive the jeep." So they decided that the designated drivers from each crew would have a race around the trailer perimeter road, (probably a half mile) and whoever had the best time would be declared the winner. They tried to start the jeep but the battery was dead, probably left something on after they stole it, so they conned the blue bus driver to give them a push and the jeep started right up. To make a long story short, after several laps a winner was declared and the boys asked, "What do we do with this jeep now?" Someone said "After we wipe off our fingerprints, let's go park it in front of the colonels' trailers." So they did...the next afternoon when they went to fly, the jeep was gone.

They found out later through confidential sources that one of the colonels who drove the jeep often partook of several adult beverages (sometimes too many), thought that perhaps he had left it downtown at a bar that he frequented...he never reported it missing with the hope it would show up...and it did. The same source stated after finding it he was one very happy colonel. As a post script, according to crew dog folk lore, the jeep was allegedly stolen from the Army detachment at Sattahib and disguised to look like an USAF vehicle…it wasn't on the Air Force books…it was apparently shared among the colonels that lived in the VIP trailers…how the colonels got it was never explained.

Chapter Eleven: Arc Light Four – "Sluggo's First Crew"

Capt Sluggo returned home and as promised, got his very own BUFF crew, a fine bunch of guys. Sluggo...aircraft commander — AC (add an e and you get ace)... how impressive. His radar navigator (bomb aimer), call sign "Mac" had one black eyebrow and one white eyebrow, unique. His copilot lived up to his call sign "Big Dave", a strapping lad. His gunner "GUNS" was a grizzled Master Sergeant, a very professional and serious guy. B-52 crews were made up of five officers and one enlisted gunner who lived in the rear end of the airplane in his own little world with his four 50 caliber guns. The other two crew dogs were the NAV and the EW, (often called the "nose picker" because he didn't have a lot to do but pick his nose until they were in hostile territory). More about the "crew concept" to follow.

When General Curtis LeMay was appointed CINCSAC he transformed a rag tag WW II bomber group into a force to be reckoned with. Over the formative years, SAC went from a force of 279 aircraft to a force of 3,207 including their own fighters. A vital part of this transformation was the integrated crew concept; crews trained to a very high degree of proficiency and standardization. The near draconian training standards led to a highly professional and capable force. It was almost like getting married, the crew lived together (especially on alert or when deployed), ate together, trained together, did off duty things together, played together, flew together, and became a true social unit. The aircraft commander assumed the role of pilot, crew leader, advisor, father confessor, friend, and at times disciplinarian (new Sluggo responsibilities for sure).

So back to the daily grind, Sluggo and crew staying combat ready, lots of ground training, flying, and nuclear alert. Preparing for the three initials that chilled the hearts of all SAC crew dogs, the ORI...Operational Readiness Inspection. When a base was in the ORI window, an unannounced group of SAC trained killer inspectors could descend on the wing at any time like a plague of locusts. Often the only notice would be an unidentified group of aircraft requesting permission to land at your base. During the ORI, the Wing was raised to the highest level of readiness simulating a nuclear war footing in which every element, ground and air, was inspected and tested including force and nuclear weapons generation, minimum interval takeoff, combat navigation, aerial refueling, low-level bombing, gunnery, and piloting in simulated emergency combat conditions. Woe to any SAC Wing King that screwed up an ORI or as the saying went; he would be "off the base by sundown" and would be forever known in the USAF as a "sundowner."

Sluggo and his band of merry men and the Wing passed the ORI with flying colors. Time to relax and recover, but wait, the Arc Light was still burning bright. And, you guessed it, the time was right for the rookie crew to go back to war. Off to training and South East Asia. Most of the

crew had been there before except the NAV and the CP who were FNG's (Blank New Guys). They were flying the B-52 D model, the workhorse of the Arc Light operation. The D model was configured for combat operations in SEA. Modifications included the "Big Belly Mod" expanding the bomb bay to carry 84 Mark 82 500-pound bombs combined with the 24 Mark 117 750-pound bombs carried on external wing racks for a grand total of 108 weapons. As they flew in three or six ship cells, you can only imagine the destructive firepower. The D's were also configured with electronic counter measures (ECM) designed to combat the older soviet Surface to Air Missiles (SAMs) and AAA that were common in SEA. The usual rotation was a month or so flying from Guam (subject of another chapter), Okinawa (another chapter), and Thailand (yet another chapter) until your 179 days were over (179 days was the longest period of time a GI could be on temporary duty).

The tour was going well, however there were several interesting incidents; a couple of them follow.

On Guam, the crews lived-in three-story barracks, two large rooms with three beds and lockers on each side with one crapper, one shower, and two sinks in between. Rather homey. One late afternoon on a no-fly day after several adult beverages and some cheap vodka that was on sale at the club, for some reason, that neither can remember, the RN and the EW got into spat complete with growling and shoving, but no punches were thrown. One snarled and threw the other's clothes from his locker over the balcony to the ground (they were on the second floor). In kind, the other threw the other's clothes over the balcony. Suddenly, Sluggo was thrown in a new role of a referee and peacemaker, so he did. After some slurred babbling by both, the event was soon over and sealed with a handshake and a hug. Sluggo thought, that went well. Then there was the NAV who took incredibly long showers and other bathroom activities, in the single shower/pooper room with the doors locked. Often, they had to pound on the bathroom doors to remind him there were five others who needed to get in. What was he doing so long in there...I wonder?

Flying out of Thailand the crews lived in prefab trailers, one bedroom with bunks on each end with a john in the middle. Usually the crew divided up with the CP and EW in one room and the NAV and RN in the other. The pilot had a room to himself...perks. The gunner slept in the gunner's barracks nearby. One morning, the boys had been selected to fly the dawn patrol. At 0 dark thirty, about 3 am, the crew bus arrived to pick up all three crews who were flying on that mission (remember they usually flew in three ship formations). The boys loaded up their gear (they had to carry cold weather stuff even though it was a zillion degree outside, in case they lost cabin pressure in flight, which was not a reason to abort the mission) and motored over to the gunners' pad to pick them up. Out came GUNS number one, soon followed by GUNS number two...but no GUNS Sluggo. The other two gunners went to look for him, they found him in the john sound asleep on the crapper with his flight suit around his ankles, they woke him up and he joined them yawning, his brother gunners tried to cover up the facts and said he was just in the bathroom doing something but he fessed up to the real story... good man...took him a long time to live that down...if he ever did.

Last story, flying out of Thailand again. They landed from a bombing mission around six pm, debriefing then off to the O Club for some eats and cheer. For some unknown reason, and since we were not flying again for about 36 hours, the CP, you remember "Big Dave," decided to tie one on. They went to the bar after dinner and the CP started really firing them down. Well into his cups, Big Dave decided to retire for the evening and headed out for his trailer. Picture this, an area bigger than a football field with probably 40 or so identical looking trailers. What you probably figured out by now, Big Dave picked the wrong trailer. What you didn't know is the CP was trying to be quiet so as not to wake up his roommate, the EW. So, he peeled off all his clothes in the dark (no PJ's for big Dave) and climbed into the top bunk. And you guessed it...it was occupied. Big Dave let out a roar and proceeded to throw the other poor sleeping crew dog to the ground all the time screaming, "What the hell are you doing in my bunk!" After the lights came on, Big Dave ate crow and was led staggering back to his real trailer. It didn't take long for the story to get out, as they knew well the crew who lived in that trailer and they were itching to tell the tale and poke Sluggo's crew in the eye...which they did...much to Big Dave's embarrassment. You can be assured, that crew probably double checked and locked their trailer doors following this adventure to keep Big Dave out.

Sluggo and the boys rotated back to Guam to finish their 179 days in paradise and prepared to return to home sweet home. On their last mission they put all the junk that they didn't want to take home into the bomb bay, old jocks, sneakers, things they didn't want their wives to see. etc., you get the idea, as a present to drop on Charlie along with the bombs.

It was revealed that their Squadron at home would be converting from the B-52 D model, the workhorse of the SAC bombing effort, to the new and improved B-52 G model BUFF. It appeared that the Arc Light

was fading and sputtering out as the B-52 G was neither flying in SEA, nor specially configured for the conventional bombing mission.

The B-52 G appeared similar to the D but it was nearly a totally different aircraft. Visibly it looked different, eight feet of the tail (vertical stabilizer to you purists) was cut off, the massive drop tanks of the older models were replaced with smaller non droppable tanks, the ailerons were removed in favor of better designed spoilers (the D had both ailerons and spoilers), the gunner's cockpit in the tail was removed and the gunner moved to the crew compartment with an ejection seat across from the EW with CTV and radar linked to the guns. The cockpit was redesigned for more crew comfort (most pilots who flew the "tall tails" ended up with bad backs, including Sluggo). The G had more powerful motors that burned less fuel; it also carried more gas topping the scales at 488,000 lbs. fully loaded, as opposed to the "tall tails" at 400,000 lbs., the wing tank bladders of the older models were replaced by wet wing fuel tanks, all these things saved considerable empty weight. A G model BUFF once flew 10,000 miles in almost 20 hours without air refueling. There were other significant changes too numerous to mention.

"Life is good" said Sluggo and his crew as they flew home.

Sluggo and his boys returned from Arc Light and pulled their first

alert tour in six months in the newly assigned B-52 G model. During the first morning preflight, Sluggo's RN, call sign McGoo, pulled him aside and said, "You've got to see this," and took him into the bomb bay where there reposed the mother of all nukes. Sluggo knew that was his weapons load but he'd never seen one in person. It was a MK/B53, "bunker buster," nine megatons and nearly 9,000 lbs. It was so big the BUFF could only carry one, it was strapped in its rack by steel cables. When the bomb was dropped, a cable cutting assembly would explosively fire titanium knife blades to cut the cables. McGoo said, "that's one big butt ugly bomb," Sluggo agreed whole-heartedly. Also, in the space in the bomb bay that was left, there

nested (pun) four cute little Quail missiles. The jet powered GAM 72 was 13 feet long and its plywood wings when deployed measured five feet. The plan was to launch these babies over enemy territory where they would fly around on a preprogramed profile simulating a BUFF with a near same radar cross

section…fool you once Ivan, fool you three more times (we hope).

Will the boys be Arc Lighting again any time soon…what do you think?

Chapter Twelve: Operation Bullet Shot – "You've Got to be Tough to Fly the Heavies"

Sluggo and crew were becoming comfortable in the new aircraft, the B-52 G model. The G had systems that the old D had never imagined. Now for the flying part, the G flew somewhat differently than the "tall tails"…but deep down inside it was still a BUFF. Some differences between the two models were discussed in the previous chapter, but here's a few more. Most of the systems on the old BUFFs (B-52 C, D, E, and F models) ran on hot gas commonly known as engine bleed air. From 300 degrees and 50 psi to 650 degrees and 160 psi, depending on the use. Sensors were located throughout the aircraft to detect a bleed air malfunction; an emergency connected to a hot gas leak was "land as soon as practicable" (SAC crew dogs were quite familiar with hot air). As the story goes, during an Arc Light mission, a crew experienced a bleed air leak warning indication in the bomb bay, after an emergency landing it was so hot in the bomb bay that the melted Tritonal explosive was leaking out of the bomb fuse threads. The G model replaced the 10 bleed air driven hydraulic packs with six engine powered hydraulic pumps, likewise, four generators replaced the four air driven alternators making the aircraft much safer. However, hot gas is still around (not only in airplanes), air conditioning and pressurization systems on almost all military and commercial jet aircraft including the B-52 to this day are still powered by bleed air. Vast improvements over the "tall tails," but alas, the G still had the dreaded water injection system for takeoff.

The boys were declared "combat ready" in the G and assumed nuclear alert with a vast array of new weapons (also discussed in the previous chapter). Things were going swimmingly well with a new CP and NAV to break in, both sharp guys. Sluggo began the process of checking out as an instructor pilot which he accomplished with flying (pun) colors. The rest of the crew followed suit becoming an all instructor crew and later their crew status was upgraded to "Select." SAC crews were designated "N" or non-ready, "R" or combat ready, "E" or highly capable and "S" elitist status, all crews strived for "S" but only a few made it. Sluggo really enjoyed instructing and excelled at it, a lot of his flying now consisted of pilot proficiency instructional missions, which was fine with him. As time went by, the "Arc Light' was a slight glow and a fond but distant memory.

Soon Sluggo was selected to attend the Central Flight Instructor Course (CFIC); the B-52 and KC-135 "Top Gun" school flying E and F model BUFFs. As discussed by a former CFIC Bomber Branch Chief, "The curriculum was the creation of men who had their turn in the meat grinder and understood the need of blood, sweat, and tears during training to forge aircrews to have the confidence and skills to do anything...and how not to get killed by students." The program consisted of academics and of course flying, but flying the BUFF and Tanker in ways you didn't think were possible. "Awesome," said Sluggo, "That's my goal, to someday be a B-52 "Top Gun" instructor at CFIC."

Soon graduation from the best flying course Sluggo had ever attended, then back home to lead the life of a SAC crew dog, training, alert, flying, training, flying, alert, flying, alert, training,...you get the idea.

Sluggo and his boys were intensely interested in the peace talks in Paris with the North Vietnamese, and in 1971 it appeared that they might result in a possible agreement. Accordingly, as a demonstration of good faith, President Nixon ordered a reduction in the aggressive air campaign and cut Arc Light sorties to 1,000 per month...was the Arc Light dimming? It appeared the bad guys thought so. "Now I'm thinking, since the U.S. has reduced the bombing pressure, let us increase our ops tempo and infiltrate more troops and equipment into the South...and then see what they do," said Uncle Ho.

One day back home, Sluggo and crew on alert detected a disturbance in the force. Lots of after-hours fluttering around going on at Wing Headquarters and the Command Post. Soon the word came down from on high, "All crew dogs will assemble for an important announcement."  Which went something like this, "Pack your bags for 179 days, due to deteriorating conditions in SEA, President Nixon has directed SAC to deploy 100 B-52 G's to Guam...and the operation will be called "Bullet Shot" and you're it." So Bullet Shot, the red headed stepchild of Arc Light was born. Sluggo and crew thought the G isn't well configured for the conventional bombing mission in SEA, the ECM is wrong and it holds only 27 iron bombs in the bomb bay and none on the wings as opposed to the D's 108, also since the gunner is now up front you lose a set of eyes in the back checking for SAMs, other aircraft, "So what? The G's are going anyway."

The boys were selected to fly one of the Wing's G's to Guam. The base gave them a great sendoff, a standing ovation...cheering as they blasted off down the runway into the wild blue yonder. During mission planning, they thought great, we'll have to stop in Hawaii for gas and spend the night...not so fast guys...we don't want no stinkin' BUFFs in Hawaii. So they hit a tanker over the Pacific and non-stopped it to Andersen AFB Guam. To say Andersen was a giant goat rope was putting it mildly. Over 150 bombers and other aircraft on the Rock and over 12,000

crew dogs, staff pukes, maintainers, bomb loaders and gassers living in tent and tin cities all over the base. Lucky crew dogs got the barracks. Since Sluggo and crew were heavy on Arc Light experience, they usually led the three ship G cells on bombing missions in South Viet Nam, Laos, and Cambodia...yes Cambodia. To break an NVA offensive in spring 1972, SAC was now flying over 3,000 bombing sorties a month.

Sluggo's copilot was yearning for his own call sign, after much thinking and trial and error, Sluggo bestowed upon him the call sign "Wedge"...the simplest tool known to man, and to his chagrin he was thereafter known as Wedge (which he secretly liked).

The G's flying out of Guam could make the mission roundtrip without air refueling, alas no U Tapao or Kadena fun for the G guys. On long boring flights back to the Rock, crews had little to do to pass the time, cassette tape decks had been installed by the EW's seat to record critical phases of the mission, no flight recorders in the BUFF. Crews soon figured out how to play music over the aircraft intercom system so the "BUFF In-Flight Entertainment System was born"...but alas no movies. One three ship group that usually flew together came up with the idea to play Bingo with the three crews over the air on a discrete frequency on the way back to the Rock. So "Bullet Shot Bingo" was hatched...can't imagine what the

Soviet and other SIGINT weenies thought when they heard B-14, N-42, O-72 and Bingo blasting over the airwaves...Ivan mused, "Some new code, I don't understand, but what does it mean and can we break it?"

One evening Captain Sluggo was leading a three-ship formation of G's back to Guam after completing a bombing sortie in Vietnam. It was a clear, dark, and moonless night; they were flying above 40,000 feet somewhere between the Philippines and Guam. As a matter of fact, of the eighteen crew dogs in the three aircraft, maybe six were awake, a pilot and a navigator in each plane as it was standard practice to take turns sleeping during the return trip of the twelve plus hour combat mission. It was Sluggo's turn to be awake and his copilot was sacked out on the floor behind the cockpit.

As he gazed out the cockpit window, he noticed the blinking lights of another aircraft far off in the distance...it appeared to be heading his way. He knew there were no other B-52 cells in their area and was doubtful that any other aircraft would be at their altitude. The longer he looked the more he believed there was another airplane out there. Sluggo called his radar nav, McGoo, down in the basement on intercom, told him about the other aircraft, and asked him to check his radar for any traffic, he said there was nothing on his scope. He took his radar out to maximum range and still nothing. Sluggo called the number two aircraft and he said he could see the lights but had nothing on his radar either, number three echoed that. He woke up Wedge and asked him to get back in his seat, after strapping in he saw the lights too. Sluggo radioed the formation and told them to turn right ten degrees, to his surprise it appeared the unknown aircraft was turning with them.

By this time everyone in all three aircraft was awake, wondering what was going on, looking out the cockpit windows, and checking their radar and flight planning information. Determined to get out of this guy's way, he directed a turn of ten more degrees right, once again the unknown seemed to turn with them, so he called for thirty degrees left followed by a turn back right to the original heading. Once again, the bogie seemed to stay with them. Halfway through the turns, an unidentified voice boomed over the radios..."Congratulations pilot, you've taken evasive action on the planet Venus." It took many rounds on Sluggo at the club to live that one down.

Time flies and 179 days came and went and the Sluggo team returned to the world...but wait, this time for only 45 some days, then back to Guam for more Bullet Shot's. While at home, Sluggo did get recurrent on all the instructor pilot stuff like low level, touch and gos, and air refueling stuff that he hadn't done in six months on Guam.

Chapter Thirteen: Linebacker II – "You Can Always Go...Downtown"

Back at Andersen AFB, things had improved, but it was still a zoo with everyone working and flying their asses off; back to bombs on target for the crew dogs. Sluggo now had over 400 BUFF combat missions. Again, the boys detected a disturbance in the force (never a good thing for crew dogs), in this case Eighth Air Force, the rumor monster was running untamed...what was to come? The words came down from most high, SAC Headquarters, you're going North...and we don't mean to Alaska...and the operation shall be called Linebacker II and all the mission planning will be done here in Omaha, Nebraska...any questions?" Day one came with 129 B-52Ds and Gs from Guam and UT supported by over

100 other mission aircraft, in three waves at night hitting military targets in Hanoi and Haiphong. Missions were "press on" – if you could make it to the target and release you were a go regardless of any engine out or maintenance problems. Additionally, no evasive action was authorized on the bomb run prior to bombs away in an effort to reduce civilian casualties. MIGs were thought to be the

biggest threat, this turned out not to be the case, in fact, two MIGs were shot down by BUFF gunners during Linebacker II. The MIGs were used to radio altitude, heading, and airspeed back to the SAM batteries that ringed the target areas. The real threats were the SAMs; over 200 were fired on day one. Two B-52Gs and one B-52D were lost. Day two launched 93 B-52s on the same general targets, lots of SAMs fired but no BUFFs lost.

Sluggo and his boys were flying on day three, 93 B-52s, target "downtown" … same ingress, headings, altitude and timing as the first two nights, Sluggo mused, "not to be SACreligious, but who thought this up…Murphy?" The NVA were ready, the MIGs came up, radioed down their info and hauled ass, and then about 220 SAMs came up. It was a tragic day for SAC, four G models and two D models were shot down including the

number 3 aircraft in Sluggo's cell, the shrapnel from the SAM detonation was so close that Sluggo's gunner could see it on his radar. Right after bombs away in the post target turn, the EW yelled, "Pilot they are on us with a SAM uplink and launch." Sluggo began evasive action…at one

point his copilot, Wedge declared, "Pilot we're upside down." Sluggo said, "I know, almost but not quite…just hang on, that SAM isn't going to get us" and it didn't (near upside down is not a normal maneuver in the BUFF). To make matters worse the post target turn was into a 100 knot headwind (the post target turn was 90 degrees at a 60 degree bank angle… a hold-over from the SAC nuclear mission tactics to turn tail to the target to escape the blast from a nuke.) "Why are we doing this here? Last time we checked we're dropping only iron bombs," thought the boys, especially since the G ECM was less effective at high bank angles, and we can egress over water if we go straight…"we've always done it that way was the school answer."

After the losses of day three, speculation raised its ugly head…the White House wants 100 BUFFs a day over North Vietnam, and mother SAC in Omaha, USA, where all the mission planning was done, said, "Damn the SAMs, full BUFFs ahead." Crew dogs and the in-theater senior leadership were not pleased. The loss of nine B-52s with over six crew members on each plane in three days, was not acceptable. All the crew dogs thought this operation smacks highly of the "Seven P's" *Piss Poor Planning Produces Piss Poor Performance*, also many thought it was an 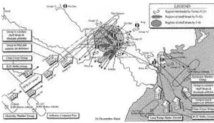 intentional show of force from the highest levels..."We'll send 100 BUFFs a night over your place and there's nothing you can do about it" (except shoot down planes). The reaction that ensued was called by some the "revolt of the generals." The stars in Guam and UT hung it out and told SAC, we can't continue to lose BUFFs at this rate, let us plan the missions...we know how to do this...we live here...this is our turf...please butt out sirs. Cool heads and common sense thankfully prevailed and special tactics were adopted and changed every night. Seven waves, 10 targets, near simultaneous time over target (TOT), different ingress and  egress routes, different altitudes and no steep post target turns...and oh, by the way, since they're shooting at us, why don't we target some SAM sites.

Sluggo and the boys were scheduled to "spare" for the launch on day seven, spares were fully loaded and crewed aircraft that could be launched as a substitute if one of the primary launch aircraft had problems or had to abort. Being a spare was not cool if you had to launch, different unplanned formations, missions, targets, etc. One of the 93 primary aircraft aborted on the runway so Charlie, the launch control colonel, radioed, "Sluggo start engines and prepare to go;" the colonel knew him and called him by name. They started engines and the number 4 motor started to choo-choo—a problem commonly known as engine compressor stalls. Sluggo radioed Charlie, "We have some engine problems, we'll have to shut down, we may need fire." Charlie said, "Roger Sluggo, you're not flying today." That's OK by us thought the crew, being a spare and launching is no fun. No BUFFs lost this night.

On Christmas Eve, SAC announced a 36 hour stand down—pro: some needed relief for air crews, ground crews, and tired airplanes—con:

let the bad guys reload. On the day after Christmas, 120 BUFFs launched, 78 took off in one batch from Guam...the largest single combat launch in SAC history. One B-52 G was lost another D damaged and crash landed at UT...but the tactics were working. The boys flew again on day 10; the target was a railroad complex on the North Vietnam/China border. Sluggo saw SAMs exploding on their launch pads or flying erratically after launch, they were almost out of SAMs, moving them down from  China and shooting without calibration. The North was in trouble. Speaking of China, Sluggo could see the lights on the ground across the border; day 10, no BUFFs lost. Day 11 came and went with no BUFFs lost. The North decided to go back to the negotiation table and sue for peace (and we all know that was just smoke and mirrors) and Linebacker II came to an end..."Way too soon," said many, "We had them on the ropes and didn't finish them." BUFFs flew 741 sorties, dropping over 15,000 tons of bombs. The price was very steep. Fifteen B-52s shot down, others damaged, crew members killed, captured, and some rescued. Twelve other supporting aircraft lost—Air Force, Navy and Marine fighters, bombers, recce and rescue. An estimated 1,240 SAMs were launched. Did the BUFFs turn the tide, no doubt; question; why didn't we do this years before? Linebacker II will always be known hereafter as SAC's 11-day war, and the common battle cry voiced by crew dogs was, "Who is SAM uplink and why is he doing these terrible things to us?" Linebacker was over; however, the Arc Light was still burning as bombing missions were resumed in South Vietnam, Laos, and Cambodia.

After the Linebacker dust settled, the powers that be pondered, we've got over 200 G crews on the Rock and only a handful of instructor pilots that are current in air refueling, touch and go landings, and other pilot stuff. Sluggo was one of the few, so his flying was soon consumed with doing pilot proficiency missions and requalifying other instructors, his forte. One bright and sunny Guamanian day, Sluggo was pulled aside by his Squadron Commander to tell him that he had received a by-name recommendation to pull a multi-year tour as an instructor at the B-52 school in California. Was Sluggo interested—what do you think? There was one formality, an interview with the school Wing Commander, a one star general, to do that he had to return to the States. So Sluggo was soon homeward bound...and yes, he got the job! After six years, 1,189 days deployed, over 2,300 combat hours, and 426 combat missions, the **Arc Light was at last out for Sluggo**. On August 15, 1973, after eight years and 126,615 B-52 sorties, **the Arc Light was finally out for everybody.**

Sluggo Observations: "In the old SAC with its draconian rules and attitudes when pressed to make a judgement the SAC crew dog answer was always without question, "Yes sir," there was only one way to do things...the SAC way. After many years of combat deployments and separations from loved ones and family and making split second decisions in a hostile war time environment, if asked to comment, the new answer was "Why are we doing this and what will we accomplish by doing it that way?" The BUFF crews became a tight knit unit in many respects a "family" that lived together and fought together. As the crew dogs amassed hundreds of missions, they became self-confident and capable of "bending the iron rules of SAC." If asked about repercussions from their antics the stock answer with a smile was, "What are they going to do to us...send us home?" As for the mission and flying, SAC has never had a more experienced or professional force. The old severe SAC way of doing things and multiple layers of adult leadership were long overdue for change. All in all, the positive changes of attitudes and behavior gleaned from the many years of Arc Light was to become a beneficial and wholesome transformation for SAC..."*this is not your father's SAC anymore.*"

Chapter Fourteen: B-52 School – "How Would You Like to Learn to Drive a BUFF?"

Sluggo packed his bags, and headed off to BUFF school, to start on a new adventure; teaching junior aviators how to fly the mighty (old) B-52. The BUFF school was then equipped with all "tall tail" B-52s; C models (non-flyers, not used for training), D models, leftover from Arc Light training, and E and F models (the only base in SAC still flying them). Students were learning how to fly a B-52 model that they would never fly again…not so cool, but hey. The newest G and H models were scheduled to replace the old "tall tails" in the near future when the Arc Light was finally out. Not a problem as Sluggo had flown all the above models except the newest H. Sluggo was sad to learn that the B-52 "Top Gun" school, the Central Flight Instructor Course (CFIC) had been disbanded because of the major impact of the combat requirements of Arc Light and Bullet Shot; rumor had it that it would be started up again when the war was over.

All new instructor pilots were initially assigned to the Combat Crew Training Squadron (CCTS) for initial orientation. Following that, all roads for new IPs led to the B-52 simulators (Sims) which were giant analog non-motion machines as old as the BUFFs that they simulated and flew feel-wise like a bulldozer, nothing like the real airplane. They lived in a very large building that used as much electricity as a small town. They were, however, very useful for teaching normal and emergency procedures to new pilots who had never been in the BUFF prior to their first flight. If you crashed the Sim, a loud explosive noise accompanied by flashing red lights would fill the cockpit (naturally a crash was a covert objective of many a crew dog at the end of a Sim ride just to see the crescendo). Full motion and visual digital Sims were on the way soon…so the man promised…however, not in Sluggo's flying lifetime. After a couple of months, some flights and many Sim instructional sessions taught by Sluggo, his boss asked him if he would like to take a train ride – SAC had a railroad?

SAC indeed had a railroad. Since all SAC bases didn't have a B-52 simulator some creative thinker posed, "Let us build some Sims, put them  on railroad cars, move them around from base to base, and call them the USAF/SAC B-52 Mobile Simulator Trains." Each train consisted of an administration car, two B-52 cars with the simulator, and a crew car. The cars were heavy at 180 tons, had expandable sides at the cockpit section and cabinets that housed the vast array of electronics and electro-mechanical servo systems that made the Sim operate. The cars traveled on regular freight trains and were escorted by the SAC NCO personnel that operated them; the instructor pilots didn't ride the rails but met the train at the appropriate base.

Sluggo departed for a month to a northern tier base that flew B-52 H models (remember Sluggo had never flown the H.) When he pointed that out, his boss said, "Don't worry about that, the systems are nearly all the same as the G model and you've flown it, and remember, a BUFF is a BUFF is a BUFF." On his first instructional Sim mission up north, the pilot asked Sluggo, "Do you want us to use ESP for takeoff?" Sluggo thought to himself, what a wise ass and said, "use whatever you want." After the ride was over, he thought they were really good guys and wondered what the ESP comment was all about. After some research, Sluggo learned ESP was the acronym for Engine Stall Prevention, a system unique to the H model and the T-33 fan jet engine, "an engine stall prevention system is provided to control the engine compressor bleed surge valves for prevention of stalls which are caused by crosswinds during ground operation...the ESP switch is located on the pilot's control wheels." Well, egg on Sluggo's face.

Time went by and after a few beers at the club with the pilots after Sim duty hours, several of them asked, "Can we bring our wives out here after you guys have no scheduled missions and let them see the Sim?" Since Sluggo was the rankest officer, he said, "Sure, let's do it." So the squadron wives, girlfriends, and whatever's, with their pilot significant others got to fly the BUFF Sim. "Lots of fun, good beer and lots of crashes and red lights and noise," thought Sluggo as he staggered back to the BOQ. On the last day of the trip, the squadron commander thanked the Sim crew and Sluggo and said, "Appreciate your efforts, especially the after-hours activities that really meant a lot to the crew dogs and their families... the snow will be coming soon, be advised your month here was our entire summer, come back any time." That was the exhausted Sluggo's last ride on the SAC railroad—tough duty?—now back to the BUFF school house.

After a few more months in the Sim, Sluggo's boss approached him "it's been great working with you but you've got a decision to make, stay here in the Sim, go to the big school house and teach BUFF academics, or go to the line squadron and teach pilots how to fly the aircraft." Sluggo thought for about five seconds and said, "nothing against you or the schoolhouse, but I think the line is the best place for me." The colonel said, "I thought you'd say that, and you will be great down there ...best of luck." Sluggo saluted smartly and thanked him and off he went to begin another new adventure.

The flying squadron was located across the street from the B-52 parking area. It was always great to greet the morning with the heavenly aroma of burning JP-4 (jet gas). The building was laid out with office space for the heavy breathers and admin weenies, a large briefing room, and multiple mission planning and debriefing rooms each large enough to hold around 20 folks all equipped with beautiful government gray metal chipped furniture (more about the furniture later). The SAC crew concept didn't really apply to the instructor dogs since there was no nuclear alert at the base and no complete crews, there were however nuclear weapons in the "bomb dump" across the runway from the base proper. The wing was responsible to generate nuclear armed bombers and crews...when and if the Russians got to the downtown mall. Just a joke, the base was not considered for a full Operational Readiness Inspection (ORI) like a normal SAC base, but a modified version called a "Buy None"...it was still serious business, and a possible career breaker for senior management, more about that later.

The instructor crews consisted of an IP, instructor radar navigator (IRN), instructor electronic warfare officer (IEW) and an instructor gunner (IG). Five or so instructor crews were assigned under a flight commander usually a major reporting to the squadron commander. The student crew was usually a student pilot, a copilot (or if no pilot was slated sometimes two copilots,) a student NAV and RN, a student EW and a gunner...a full airplane, 10 bodies, four fully qualified SAC trained killers and six aspiring ones...for the record, the instructor positions had no ejection seats; to bail out you jumped through any available hole.

For the next few months these fine new guys (FNG's) would be taught to fly and love the BUFF...and at times, try to kill their instructors. Sluggo would fly in either the right seat or the left depending who was being trained, a pilot or a copilot, a normal mission was seven or so hours long; takeoff, air refueling, navigation, low level and back home for approaches, pattern work, touch and go landings and ending with a full stop, lots of fun. He especially liked the two copilot crews because he could teach them pilot things like air refueling that copilots wouldn't normally get with a student pilot crew, and that's the way that Sluggo started back in the day.

The B-52 copilot had his hands full of duties. Up until the BUFF, big complex aircraft had flight engineers to handle the numerous systems that kept the thing running. In the bomber as well as flying, the copilot was also the flight engineer responsible for keeping gas flowing to the engines and the airplane in balance from the myriad of fuel tanks and if flying with missiles (Hell Dogs) keeping those babies running. If that wasn't enough, the CP was also responsible for the AC and DC electrical systems, cabin pressurization and air conditioning, engine starting systems, the dreaded missiles and lots of other stuff.

During the navigation leg of a two-copilot flight (both 2 Lts) Sluggo had to pee so he put one copilot in the pilot seat with the other in the copilot seat. He rushed downstairs to relieve himself, when he came back upstairs the copilots were laughing. Sluggo asked, "What's so funny?" They replied, "We wondered if you would trust the two of us to fly the aircraft, or pee your pants."

For the most part all the pilots were decent sticks, however Sluggo had one copilot who was really bad. He mused, "how did this guy make it through pilot training?" During discussions with Sluggo, the student said that before he came in the AF he was an ambulance driver and that was his forte and he really enjoyed it, wow! On one flight in the traffic pattern with an instrument approach to a touch and go landing, the young lad was flying and doing a great job, right on airspeed, heading and glide path, Sluggo thought to himself, "Boy, thanks to your great instruction this guy's really doing great, I'm one hell of an IP." About 10 feet above the ground the copilot let go of the airplane, threw his arms in the air and moaned, "I just can't land this airplane." Sluggo grabbed the plane in an attempt to recover and smote the runway several mighty blows, take that runway, and that, and, that...you get the idea. It was very silent in the airplane during most of the next pattern to a full stop landing made by Sluggo, "I was really complacent, never again," thought Sluggo, "I guess he can always go drive Air Force ambulances if he doesn't make it through here." The airplane was slightly bruised (tires) but not hurt. The guy said he was sorry for his stupid move; he did finally graduate...but barely.

And now some tales of the squadron. A SAC bomb squadron commander was traditionally a Lt Col pilot. SAC decided to diversify and appointed the first navigator squadron commander. Sluggo knew him fairly well and had flown with him numerous times, he was a good guy albeit overly serious at times. After taking over, he thought that the squadron instructors looked a little scruffy...and alas, Sluggo thought he was right. So he directed that once every two weeks there would be an open ranks inspection wearing the duty uniform, no green bags (flight suits) please. The troops got rebellious, especially the pilots...but life goes on. Only a few could remember the process of an open ranks inspection so a little study was required.

On the blessed day the squadron smartly assembled in the parking lot for the ordeal. One of the pilots was a very hairy man (call sign Mook) and ample tufts of chest hair were protruding from the top of his tee shirt. The new commander stopped in front of him, checked him out and requested that at the next inspection he be prepared to cite chapter and verse of AF regulations concerning body hair. The group could have erupted in laughter but held it in with only a few snickers. At the next formation, when it was his turn to be inspected, Mook answered the CO's request and replied "Sir, regulations state body hair cannot be braided, dyed or adorned, other than that no other restrictions." Once again the group almost lost it. Several other of the squadron dissidents (shocking, Sluggo was not one of them), all pilots of course, as planned, showed up with little patches of fake chest hair protruding from their tee shirts. Everyone again nearly lost it and that my friends, was the end of inspections for quite some time.

A couple of days later the CO called Sluggo into his office and told him to close the door. Addressing him by his first name he asked, "What should I do about these pilots?" Sluggo said, "Sir you've got to remember most of them recently returned from years of combat...as the first navigator CO, I think they were just testing you and I believe you passed by not making a big deal out of their antics, they're all good crew dogs and things will be fine." So he cooled it as if nothing had happened, things soon returned to normal, and life was good.

The squadron was prime for a "Buy None," a mini ORI, a pass or die inspection if you will, rumor had it that it would be the following Monday. Some great brain suggested that the squadron furniture looked really bad and should be painted. So, a mandatory Saturday painting party was declared. The maintenance shop provided some very attractive dark blue metallic paint. The work started at the crack of dawn in the parking lot and finished before sundown. All the slightly tacky furniture was moved back into the building. As predicted, the "Buy None" struck on Monday, and yes, you guessed it, the furniture was still wet and very tacky and the CO was near to a stroke...thankfully the Inspectors didn't sit on them and didn't really notice, and if they did they didn't say anything...the furniture eventually dried in four or five days.

A significant part of the exercise was generation of the BUFFs to a wartime footing, this involved loading nuclear weapons on the planes and

putting them on combat alert status. Sluggo and his boys were selected; oh joy, to generate one of the airplanes complete with four B-28 thermonuclear bombs. During the preflight, the RN and NAV who were responsible for inspecting the weapons discretely came up to Sluggo and whispered, "There's something leaking out of one of the bombs." "You've got to be "shitting" me," was his response. They all crept into the bomb bay and sure enough there was some liquid in a seam that ran around the side of the bomb. They all scratched their heads remembering nuclear weapons school, "I don't think that there is any liquid inside that thing," they mused. Remember the inspectors were watching this from afar. Sluggo went up to the crew chief and asked him to get his chief over.

To make a long story short he called his chief, who called his chief and his chief and so on. Soon there was a gathering of eagles and blue staff cars and trucks and lots of toing and froing. The munitions commander showed up and confirmed with Sluggo and crew  there was no liquid in the nuke. After much discussion they closely inspected the bomb bay and discovered one of the two BUFF flap motors that were located way up in the top of the bomb bay was weeping a minute quantity of oil. The oil was seeping unseen down the struts and bomb rack and into the seam around the bomb. By this time quite a mob had gathered including all the Wing big boys. Sluggo said, "Since we're simulating wartime rules, and this airplane is fully capable of combat, I have no problem accepting it, my crew and I will fly this bird as is." After intense deliberation, everyone agreed that was acceptable, including the inspectors…oh happy day. The Wing passed the "Buy None."

Lots of changes were in the air (pun) at the BUFF school. The Wing fully converted from the old "tall tail" B-52s to the newest and greatest G and H models. As discussed earlier,  Sluggo had flown the G but not the mighty H.

A decision was made at the highest levels to reactivate the BUFF and Tanker "Top Gun" school since the Arc Light had at long last burned out. So CFIC was going to be reborn. There were only a few old fart instructors left from the original school, but not many and they were quite senior, so bids were opened to select a new cadre. Sluggo jumped on that as being a CFIC instructor was an ultimate goal in his B-52 life. Soon a selection

process began with interviews and proficiency flights with the old farts…
will Sluggo make the grade? I wonder. Oh, I forgot, sometime during this
discourse, Sluggo attained the rank of Major and was waiting to pin them
on…Sluggo mused, "I thought I was on my way to be a Captain for life."

Chapter Fifteen: Top Gun School – "Can a BUFF and a Tanker Really Do That?"

Being selected for the rebirth of CFIC was an ultimate goal of Sluggo's B-52 life – will he make the grade, I wonder?

He made it! Hooray, selected for the new CFIC cadre…the beginning of a new chapter in the Sluggo flying book. Now for some great aviating…but not so fast hotshot, the new course doesn't exist yet…and you and your flying mates are going to build it. And so it began. Since the school wasn't officially stood up, lots of late hours and weekends to develop both the flying and academic curriculum. The school wasn't only for pilots, but all crew positions, NAV, EW, Gunner, Boom Operator, in both the B-52 and the KC-135. Since the "students" were all experienced crew dogs at their specialties desiring to upgrade to instructor status, the term "student" was replaced by the title "instructor candidate (IC)." In fact, to become an instructor in any tactical SAC aircraft (U-2, SR-71, T-39, etc.) you were required to attend at least the non-flying, academic portion of CFIC.

The powers that be gave CFIC a newly remodeled building which was quite adequate for their needs and actually near perfect, "Seems like mother SAC is serious about this," thought Sluggo, relieved them from previous duties and formed the gaggle into instructor crews. CFIC consisted of a Lt Col Chief, a Major Bomber Branch Chief with six instructor crews, a Major Tanker Branch Chief with six instructor crews, and a small admin staff for a total of over 40 aviators and four paper pushers, and they were  ones always overworked and, I might add, having to put up with all those airplane guys. Getting ready for the first class, the boys (there were not any girls flying in the AF in those days, alas) redefined the academics, including flight characteristics, aerodynamics, principles of instruction, navigation, air refueling, emergency procedures, you get the idea, and practiced and refined the flying mission scenarios and dry ran it all over and over again. Bombers and Tankers were mixed together in large bull pen areas each crew dog with his own small desk…"Wow," thought Sluggo, "I've been in the Air Force for 10 years and this is the first time I've had my very own desk …I hope this is not an omen of things to come, I think I'd rather fly an airplane than this ugly grey scratched up thing with drawers and no motors." So my friends, think about it, BUFF and TIF crew dogs in a large room with grey desks, living together in perfect harmony…what a unique concept.

Now a bit of purpose. The objective of CFIC was to develop a course of instruction which would provide a cadre of highly effective instructors who in turn, would provide a highly trained crew force for SAC. The motto of CFIC was *"Fly the Aircraft."* Quote, "These three simple words are the philosophy and purpose of CFIC. Critical or multiple emergencies place unique demands on all crew members. In a situation of extreme stress, it may appear that conditions exceed the aircrew's capabilities. You can and may easily become distracted from your primary duty of controlling the aircraft. In an emergency situation, perform that procedure which will best counter the most critical emergency. That procedure is to check the aircraft's flying condition. The first item must be airspeed, literally the breath of life…a safe airspeed will keep the aircraft flying. Then check the power setting, altitude, and attitude. This is what we mean by *Flying the Aircraft.* Take other necessary actions only after flying conditions are under control. You must develop this mental attitude and preach it to other crew members who you will influence as an instructor."

Kind of a long quote but that was what the course was all about, in unusual aviation situations, the normal way may not be the sure way to save your butt, and sometimes unusual extraordinary actions not clearly explained in the "book" may be required…and if you don't know how to execute these extraordinary actions your ass may be grass and Murphy may be a John Deere. In those regards, CFIC was not an easy course, it was a very demanding and intense course of instruction and stressed the limits of both the aircraft and the air crew…"Fly it until the last piece stops moving." But all work and no play make the crew dog a dull boy, so as you will soon see, it was also a fun course.

The official description of the CFIC patch was the mailed fist of SAC holding down a Soviet missile…the unofficial description was something else…enough said.

The Chief, call sign "Lucky" informed us that we would soon be formalizing the academic portion of the school and assigning primary instructors to the courses. They included Aerodynamics, Instruments, Principles of Instructions, Emergency Procedures, Mission Planning, Navigation, et. al, you get the idea. Sluggo was flying the day when the class instructors would be named; Lucky assured him, "Don't worry while you're out slipping the surly bonds, we'll assign you a course that will be right up your alley." The next day when he went back to work there was a big sign on his grey desk that said, "Congratulations Sluggo, you're the aerodynamics instructor." Lucky laughed and said, "You weren't here and no one else wanted it, so my friend, you were selected…if you snooze, you lose." Sluggo thought, "Aerodynamics was never my strong suit but I think I know how airplanes fly, so my course will cover practical things you should know to keep from busting your ass, or better said, *Aero for Dummies*."

And soon the great day arrived, welcoming the first class, followed by day one of academics, scary. One of the CFIC BUFF NAVs was so nervous about teaching his first class that he locked himself in a stall in the head and drank a can of Coors…his class went great. Class size was usually around 60 plus, all crew specialties both bomber and tanker at first, then breaking down into specifics, pilots, NAVs, etc. So Sluggo, with a serious face, walked into the first pilot Aero Class, introduced himself and flipped a slide on the screen and said, "When this course is over, by comprehending these formulas, you will understand how your aircraft flies." Sluggo then looked around the room and observed the agony on the IC's faces.

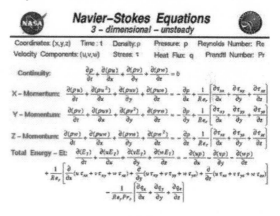

After a pause he said, "just kidding, but there are some important basic principles that I want to get across in this Aero Course. Here's a few:
- *Pull back on the stick and the buildings get smaller…continue to pull back on the stick and the buildings get bigger.*

- *The airplane knows what it can and what it can't do…be sure you know that too…therefore, don't put the machine in any attitude that it doesn't know and understand.*
- *Ground effect is your friend most of the time.*
- *The runway in front of you is your friend…the runway behind you is usually not your friend.*
- *Upon landing, keep the glass side up and the rubber side down.*
- *Fly it until the last piece stops moving.*
- *And as the old saying goes, "There's old pilots and bold pilots but no old bold pilots."*

Enough talk of academics, but before we aviate, we must mission plan and you the ICs are the instructors and we the CFIC cadre are very dumb and stupid students who quest for knowledge, so apart from us demonstrating maneuvers in flight, always consider us green students. And by the way, most of your flying will be done from the right seat (some of the ICs had never been copilots, lots of different stuff over there). Two BUFF pilot ICs would fly together with one CFIC IP. There were also common-sense judgement discussions during mission planning. For example, "We know that you're the best pilot in the world, but on a training sortie, if the weather is trashed and you get to minimums or maybe a little bit lower without seeing the runway, don't be macho and bust your ass, go around, proceed to an alternate, have a cold beer and live to fly another day…you get the idea."

So, at last, let us go fly. The normal CFIC profile was about six or so hours; takeoff, air refueling, low level, and back to the base for pattern work and landings. One of the most difficult tasks of flying the BUFF is air refueling, two big airplanes close together, going fast.

Pilots were required to refuel in any conditions, weather, night, unusual and unexpected situations. One of the key objectives of CFIC was to demonstrate to the instructor candidates that the

aircraft could safely perform air refueling in adverse conditions. One of the keys to refueling was of course the tanker pilot; his actions, airspeed, attitude, etc. multiplied the subsequent reactions of the receiver pilot by several orders of magnitude. CFIC always planned and aviated with a mated tanker. They would taxi together to the runway and takeoff in trail formation, with the BUFF 30 seconds (or less but don't tell) behind the tanker. The TIF would request MARSA (Military Assumes Responsibility for Separation of Aircraft) or "if we run into each other it's our fault...not yours," from Air Traffic Control (ATC) and off they would go. CFIC had a great rapport with ATC in the Bay Area and they weren't surprised by anything that the boys did, and often flew with them when they could. Gear up, flaps up, air refueling checklist, slipway doors open, and hook up with the tanker prior to the 15 mile turn out of traffic, and climb out and fly in contact all the way to the refueling area. Most of the ICs had never seen refueling in any condition other than straight and level flight.

While in the refueling area, the first order of business was a demonstration maneuver called the "WIFF" – a definition follows: "The Wifferdill maneuver refers to any number of fancy turns performed in an aerial flight show or while flying aggressively. It is an action with both horizontal and vertical components, usually performed at the end of one maneuver in preparation for the next. As the plane is climbing the pilot makes a turn reversal, and as the plane descends it is turned so that it can make its next maneuver. The whifferdill is a basic aerial warfare maneuver that is used to reverse course in a dogfight with very little loss of energy/airspeed. It is also a fundamental maneuver used in air shows." "Wow" said Sluggo, "so we do air show and dogfight stuff...I never thought of it that way...now it's all clear to me."

The CFIC version of the WIFF basically involved refueling while

 hooked up to the tanker executing steep turns and climbs and dives. The WIFF was a dynamic process, not just one big turn. It was a series of lazy-chandelle type maneuvers that started out small and increased with each reversal until the target attitude was achieved (or sometimes exceeded). The

purpose of the demo was to show the ICs that if the two aircraft and pilots were in sync with each other and if they both understood the aerodynamic interaction between the two jets, that nearly "any" attitude could be achieved successfully while in contact. It was a confidence and teamwork maneuver and demonstrated that actions that were not in the manual could be accomplished safely if the situation required. To say the least, it was a real eye opener to the ICs who had never seen anything like this. The secret of course was the tanker pilot, cool, calm, collected and smooth who could feel the interaction of the bomber on his jet and react accordingly. One of the CFIC tanker IPs was very big old southern boy call sign "Hormel." He had huge hands and thus was accused of being ham fisted, hence the call sign ...but he was one of the smoothest tanker drivers on earth and Sluggo's favorite to fly the WIFF with...his call sign should have been "Velvet" but that didn't quite fit.

As previously stated, the goal of CFIC was to prepare crew dogs to perform the mission regardless of the situation. An example from Desert Storm follows...due to a number of unforeseen circumstances a cell of BUFFs was running out of gas and had to chase tankers throughout the

skies to continue their mission...here's what happened, this event came just three months after the pilot returned from CFIC.

"We ended up in Iraq short on gas and carrying a load of new weapons on converted cruise missile pylons. The drag was more than expected, hence that's why we were short on gas big time, so we needed an extra refueling to make it to the post-strike base. We asked the AWACS and we got a snap vector to a group of tankers holding south of the border. Well, snap vector was not part of the SAC lexicon and neither was the anchor refueling that we headed for. I don't think anyone in BUFFs could spell anchor let alone fly it with the jets in the configuration we had. Oh, by the way did I mention it was at night and the tankers were orbiting right in the only cloud deck in this part of the world. Well, my NAVs worked their magic and got us close enough behind the tanker to make visual contact.

The whole point of this story is that we were prepared for this by the blood and sweat at CFIC. The confidence and skills that it took to do what none of us had ever done before, under the most adverse scenario you can think of, was forged by the tough curriculum at CFIC. This curriculum – including the WIFF – was the creation of men who had their turn in the meat grinder and understood the need for blood sweat and tears during training to forge aircrews who had the confidence and skills to do anything." Sluggo didn't remember the meat grinder part, but it was a very nice story that made him proud. "35 Minutes from Takeoff to Landing" describing Sluggo's craziest, action packed, and shortest, BUFF mission ever...follows. Fly Safe.

Chapter Sixteen: 35 Minutes – "Takeoff To Landing"

As much as Sluggo loved the BUFF, it could be a temperamental beast at times, and it would occasionally try to show you who was really the boss. In a departure from previous chapters, Sluggo relates his shortest flight in the bomber. The following article was printed in a SAC publication describing an adventure that he experienced back in the day. The article is presented in quotes with comments from his nibs where appropriate. Here you go:

> *"Have you ever had the feeling that "today is going to be one of those days?" Well, I would like to relate an incident, I should say a combination of incidents, that would most probably put you in this frame of mind."*

> *"At 1807 local time, on 14 February 1977, a B-52H took off from Castle AFB, CA on a routine night training mission. The crew consisted of three instructors assigned to the SAC Central Flight Instructor Course (CFIC), and two instructor pilot candidates. Captain Sluggo was the pilot in command. A short but action packed 35 minutes later this aircraft, due only to the quick and accurate responses of this very professional crew, made an uneventful emergency landing."*

SLUGGO NOTE: Sluggo had been selected for Major but hadn't pinned the gold leaves on yet. It was a CFIC night pilot proficiency mission with two IPs and an IN (minimum required crew for a BUFF flight is two pilots and a nav) and as the article stated two instructor pilot (IP) candidates both of whom were qualified B-52 aircraft commanders. (Attendance at CFIC was a mandatory SAC requirement to upgrade to IP in all tactical aircraft.) Of course, it was a night mission with air refueling and pattern and landing practice…stuff like this doesn't happen in the daytime. Also, four experienced pilots on one aircraft is asking for trouble. The article states that the emergency landing was uneventful, but I can assure you that it was anything but uneventful! **Back to the article.**

"Let me take you through the sequence of events that led to this unusually short mission! Preflight was normal through engine start. At that time, the No 7 generator required several attempts at paralleling before it would remain on line. During taxi, the bomb doors refused to close until the control circuit breakers were pulled and reset several times. During the pre-takeoff visual inspection of the aircraft, the Supervisor of Flying (SOF) discovered a large fuel leak coming from the No 6 engine. The engine was shut down and takeoff was delayed for one hour while maintenance personnel replaced a broken fuel line."

SLUGGO NOTE: All this happening on the ground should have clued us that this airplane had a bad attitude, was tired, wanted to rest, and did not want to fly that evening...and "you can't make me." Since we were so late our tanker was long gone and the mission was going to be pilot proficiency/pattern work/landings only. **Back to the article.**

"Once finally airborne the landing gear failed to retract. The crosswind crab system was cycled and the gear came up. During flap retraction, the cycle took twice the normal amount of time. The pilot advised the crew that one of the two flap motors had probably failed, this was later confirmed after landing. Shortly thereafter, the No 7 generator circuit breaker opened and would not reset. Its electrical power was now lost for the remainder of the flight. Remember the problems with that stubborn number 7 generator during the preflight. Then the number one main rudder/elevator hydraulic light came on indicating to the crew that one quarter of elevator and rudder control had been lost. Simultaneously, the number 5 generator overheat light illuminated. Unsuccessful attempts to decouple the generator necessitated the shutdown of the number 5 engine. This procedure was essential because if an overheat light illuminates, and the generator cannot be decoupled, continued operation of the engine could result in a serious inflight fire. While this was happening the number 2 main rudder/elevator hydraulic and the number 2 auxiliary rudder/elevator hydraulic lights came on. Because of the light indications the crew assumed that one quarter of rudder/elevator control remained. As we shall

soon see, this was not the case, at this time the aircraft and the crew was without any control of the rudder elevator."

SLUGGO NOTE: We climbed to 20,000 ft. and entered a holding pattern above the airdrome to collect our wits. It was a clear winter night and I could see the beautiful lighted runway below us and decided that we needed to be down there ASAP as Murphy and FUBAR were working overtime against us. The flight was beginning to resemble an emergency procedure simulator ride with one exception… the simulator was on the ground…and we were in the air. **Back to the article.**

"After two minutes, the number two auxiliary hydraulic light flickered and then went out. All of these incidents were unrelated. What would you do in this situation? How would you react?"

SLUGGO NOTE: The last series of events settled it…we're landing. I informed the command post and they told me to standby as they were discussing the situation…so I informed them we were going to make a heavyweight landing. There is no fuel dump capability in the BUFF, the only way to reduce weight is to drone around making holes in the sky and that takes time and the way stuff was breaking I wasn't sure we had much left.   If truth were known, we were probably going to be slightly above the max landing weight of 325,000 lbs. They didn't argue; they also didn't approve it, but they didn't say no, and they responded with the infamous command post reply…"standby"…plausible deniability, maybe? I heard later that they were trying to get Boeing on the line to provide expert assistance...alas, too late as I was declaring an emergency and heading down. **Back to the article.**

"Both pilots, working as a team, responded in an outstanding manner to these multiple malfunctions, with primary emphasis on "Flying the Aircraft."

A decision was made to attempt a heavyweight landing at 325,000 pounds gross weight before other malfunctions could arise. This is the maximum recommended landing weight of the B-52 and is not normally accomplished. Throughout the penetration and approach, the pilots experienced rather sluggish pitch control. It might also be pointed out that during the massive electronical malfunctions, all navigational equipment including inflight radar, TACAN and VOR failed. During the landing flare, elevator control was unexpectedly marginal. Airbrakes were required to raise the nose of the aircraft during the flare to prevent a hard landing. By this time, the attitude of the pilots was, "what more could happen?" Well, you have probably guessed it! When the drag chute lever was activated upon landing, the pilot chute came out but the main drag chute did not deploy. The pilot managed to stop the aircraft within the confines of the runway, but four brakes overheated in the process."

SLUGGO NOTE: Since we were so heavy and going so fast at landing, 160 plus, I aimed for the very end of the runway, as the old saying goes "the runway behind you is not your friend." The airplane was very sluggish (no pun) when I started the landing flare, I pulled the yoke back as far as it would go and the plane wouldn't rotate so I deployed air brakes to their maximum, the nose came up and we landed, surprising not too hard. Are we done now? Murphy said, "No." At 130 kts. we attempted to put out the drag chute and Murphy said, "not so fast big boy the chute's not coming out to play tonight" and it didn't. After touchdown, I really got on the brakes, I could hear the antiskid cycling wildly sounding like guns shooting off. I knew as a last resort, we might stop if I turned the antiskid off but the brakes would probably lock and I would for sure blow all the tires creating an even more dangerous situation with giant hunks of zillion ply rubber flying around near all the gas we still had left in the jet. I was afraid we were going to run out of runway before we got the BUFF stopped...I told the crew to lock their inertial reels and hang on. But the aircraft started to gradually slow down as the antiskid was really doing its job. We did exit the runway proper and went into the 1,000-ft. overrun, finally the BUFF stopped with a big groan, we all took a deep breath, waited until all the pieces stopped moving, shut her down, and smartly exited the aircraft...because now this turkey belonged to someone else, not me. The Wing Commander and Maintenance Colonel came zooming up in their staff cars at the end of the runway as they were waiting for us at a safe distance. As we were standing there, the Maintenance Colonel informed me that I had burned up $28,000 worth of his brakes and the Wing King remarked, "Captain do you know what the difference between a hero and a bum is?" No sir, I said, and he said, "That

600 feet of concrete overrun you've got left"—congratulatory and comforting words in Wing King speak, I guess. As we walked around to look, the brakes were smoking…dangerous…and the whole ass end of the BUFF was covered with bright red hydraulic fluid, and the little pilot chute of the large drag chute was flapping in the breeze. **Back to the article.**

"*It was later discovered that the pilot had even less control than he thought. The No. 1 auxiliary rudder/elevator was also inoperative due to complete fluid loss in the No. 1 system. The crew was unaware of this since the warning light for that system was also malfunctioning. This resulted in the rudder and elevator control being totally dependent on only one of the normal four hydraulic systems. The fact that the remaining No 2-auxiliary rudder/elevator system was operating at reduced efficiency on only windmill RPM, due to the shutdown of number 5 engine, and standby pump pressure explains the control difficulty experienced during the landing flare.*"

"*The quick and accurate responses by the pilots and the rest of the crew saved a multimillion dollar aircraft and possibly the lives of its crew members and the lives and property of other people on the ground. The two pilots agreed that this was one of the few conceivable instances when an immediate landing was warranted. The compound electrical problems combined with a rapidly deteriorating control capability contributed to their decision to land at 325,000 pounds. In most emergency situations, in B-52 aircraft, a reduction of gross weight while obtaining aid and advice from the ground agencies would be safer course of action.*"

"*It should be noted that during the final investigation, it was determined that crew could have done nothing more than they did in this situation nor should they have done anything different.*"

"*This 35-minute flight in a B-52 proved to be one of the shortest on record and also one of the most action-packed flights experienced by a CFIC crew. Tech order compliance, coupled with professional competence, made this a story that they could tell their*" *flying buddies. The entire crew should be commended for their professionalism in this very stressful situation. Thanks for a JOB WELL DONE."*

SLUGGO NOTE: Due to a previous BUFF crash with nearly the same scenario, we actually taught the rudder/elevator out landing procedure using airbrakes at CFIC. So, here's what happened concerning that earlier crash, following a myriad of poor decisions and misdirection and total FUBAR actions by numerous people on the ground, including the base Command Post, the unit Wing King, SAC, Boeing, the squadron cleaning lady, (too many cooks??) and of course Murphy. The crew attempted to land following their recommendations…which the pilot questioned, but hey, they were the experts. The pilot in command (call sign "Schultz") was a very experienced instructor and flight examiner. When he attempted to put the plane on the ground, the aircraft didn't perform on landing the way the experts said it would. He was unable to rotate the aircraft to a landing attitude. It was estimated that he hit the runway nose gear first with a force of over 13 Gs, and that contact broke

the aircraft apart at landing. The cockpit separated and rolled several thousand feet down the grass next to the runway and stopped inverted, the remainder of the aircraft tried to do a touch and go take off in the opposite direction as the engines went to full throttle when the cockpit separated. All the crew was alive and well aside from lots of aches and pains and a few cracked bones…one of the minor causalities was the navigator who released his seat belt only to fall to the floor since the BUFF cockpit was near upside down. The tough construction of the remarkable BUFF played a critical role in the survival of the crew dogs. The Air Force Flying Safety Board that was convened to investigate the accident described the incident as a "fatal crash." The responsible Wing King was fired for bad judgement…as he was making decisions based on his experience and had never flown this model BUFF which was a considerably different jet, systems wise, then the B-52s he had previously flown. **Back to the article.**

"As a post script to this narrative Sluggo was selected by Headquarters SAC together with Schultz to appear in a Video Tape Program analyzing both incidents and the series of decisions that contributed to the crash in Schultz's case, and successful landing in Sluggo's case. This presentation was distributed command wide and has been an important contribution to the training of SAC aircrews. Additionally, analysis of this incident resulted in a change in the operating procedures of the B-52 G & H aircraft, and a Technical Order (TO) modification to the rudder/elevator hydraulic systems of those models. Sluggo was also awarded an Order of Daedalians Flying Safety Award for the "best handling of an inflight emergency."

SLUGGO NOTE: The initial modification of this system was a new and improved way to fly the BUFF, an early attempt at "fly by wire." The book, known as the "Dash One" said "it's a totally redundant system, almost no chance of complete failure," Mister Murphy said, "you think totally redundant...watch this." Obviously, it still had a few bugs, and hopefully they were fixed with the TO modification. It also became the blue-plate special emergency of the day in BUFF simulator rides. The crew dogs all walked away, the BUFF was in intensive care, but not dead...ergo some skill and lots of luck, and screw Murphy. Both the BUFF and the intrepid aviators pictured here, would live to play another day.

Chapter Seventeen: More Top Gun – "BUFF Flying Doesn't Get Any Better Than This"

Flying and teaching at CFIC…life is good. We left the *Top Gun Chapter* during air refueling (AR) so that's where we'll start *More Top Gun*. One more comment about the WIFF as described in the other chapter. During the WIFF, Sluggo's favorite tanker toad, "Hormel" would make sure that Sluggo was grunting and pulling G's rolling out the bottom of

the maneuver when climbing and turning…what an ass. Pulling serious G's in a BUFF was a rush, except for all the chicken bones from old in-flight lunches that had fallen through the floor and were now floating through the cockpit as they pulled negative G's. As

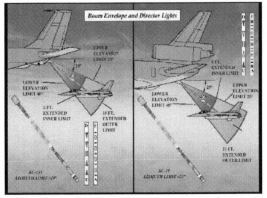

previously discussed, AR was the most difficult phase of flight for B-52 pilots to master and thus CFIC spent a lot of time on the boom instructing…an hour and a half plus was not unusual…a true physical and mental workout especially at night or in the weather.

Tankers are equipped with flight director lights on the bottom of the fuselage to assist the receiver pilot. Red, Yellow, Green, indicating up,

down, forward and aft. A natural tendency of the BUFF pilot was to chase the lights to maintain green/green, or perfect position, which just complicated the process because to pass gas you didn't have to stay perfectly green, only stay in control in the safe envelope. Accordingly, CFIC stressed using visual references on the tanker vice the director lights, you could see change on the visual picture faster than you could on the lights because the lights don't give true vertical and horizontal information but depend on up and down, and in and out movement of the boom. So, pick a visual picture on the tanker that works for you, a row of rivets, a radio antenna, an inspection plate, you get the idea.

A challenge for instructor candidates was to demonstrate the boom limits while instructing the very dumb CFIC IP students (Sluggo, et.al.) in the fine arts of refueling. One of the extremely dumb IP students claimed that the aircraft was slippery, and his hands kept sliding off the controls. After the IC racked his brains to figure out why, the "student" then held his hands up showing that his flying gloves were on backwards with the slick side in and the grip side out. Lesson...never underestimate what a student can come up with. Sluggo could run his seat all the way up, trim the BUFF, and refuel with his knees using only the throttles, demonstrating that the airplane did fine without a lot of pumping of the controls and thrashing around. Refueling would end with the impromptu demonstration of an emergency breakaway maneuver initiated by the tanker boom operator.

The basic SAC B-52 training mission was about eight to nine hours long and designed to closely simulate a typical nuclear combat sortie. As such, takeoff, air refueling, celestial navigation/missile programing leg, a high-altitude practice bomb release, dropping down into a low-level route, rumbling through hill and dale, complete with electronic counter measures and another bomb release, all scored by ground radar, at night or in the weather, no problem..."Neither snow nor rain nor heat nor gloom of night stays these aviators from the swift completion of their appointed rounds" ...quote the nuclear mailmen. Then back home for an instrument approach or two, usually to a full stop landing because only IPs were authorized to do touch and gos. The missions were tightly structured leaving little time for practice of basic airmanship. Lots of hard work and not much time for fun pilot stuff. CFIC missions didn't really fit that norm, but they did touch on the basics of the SAC combat mission as the ICs included Pilots, Navs, EWs, Gunners and Boom Operators ICs who were also being trained. Done with refueling, now off to an altitude block for some air work, and various things that might not ever be done on a basic BUFF training sortie, with the IC instructing the really stupid CFIC IP student throughout. Some of maneuvers included Vertical S/Ds, Evasive Action, Engine Shutdown and Relight, and other stuff that ICs might have only seen once or twice or never, in their BUFF careers …including initial buffet to a stall…a B-52 in a stall, now that's a shuddering thought. Done with the air work, now off to some fun at low level flying.

The B-52 was designed to be a strategic high altitude, high speed (but subsonic) nuclear bomber with extended intercontinental range capable of striking anywhere in the world with inflight air refueling. It would replace the slow B-36, a ten-engine prop and jet aircraft often called the "aluminum overcast," and the limited range six engine jet B-47 from which the BUFF was spawned. As the cold war progressed or digressed, whatever the case, surface to air missiles and other anti-aircraft stuff quickly advanced; the strategy and tactics big brains determined that the only way that bombers could survive and make it to their targets with gravity bombs would be at an extreme low altitude. The new role of the BUFF as a low-level penetrator called for structural modifications, improved

electronic countermeasures, and new equipment and instrumentation for terrain avoidance. We're talking about 500' and 350 kts – 400 mph or so in the mountains, in the weather and at night, absolutely no fun…but in the daytime in good weather, it was a blast. With the turbulence at low altitude the ride was anything but smooth, and the BUFF was often described as a million parts going different directions at the same time. The B-52 wing was very strong and flexible and could move up and down at the wingtip about 18', you could literally look out the window at low level and see the wings flapping…so calling the jet a bird was no exaggeration, at the same time you could see the engine nacelles moving in yet different directions.

Military low-level routes officially named 'Oil Burners' on aeronautical charts, were restricted zones (military aircraft only) scattered throughout the U.S. in sparsely populated places…Montana, Utah, Arizona, New Mexico, etc.…with simulated bombing targets scored by ground radar. They were typically around two hours long and included a mix of mountainous and level terrain. They were strictly controlled by

ATC. After the energy crisis in the 70's, the name was changed to 'Olive Branch' routes...political correctness even back when. Flying a big airplane fast and low to the ground in this kind of terrain demanded the utmost in coordination from the entire crew working as a team...you could bust your ass in a heartbeat...this was a key stress point at CFIC as many a BUFF crashed during low level training. So, many a crew dog would be sweating and physically whipped climbing out of the route.

One day, Sluggo and his ICs were flying a great low-level route that crested a ridge line and dived down into the east end of Lake Powell. Sluggo was in the right seat and clearing for traffic when he spotted a red

and white Cessna 172 off the right wing so close he could see that that the pilot was wearing a white shirt and dark sunglasses. As they went roaring by Sluggo thought this guy will hit our jet wash and could end up a smoking hole in the ground. They called ATC and reported the incident, ATC called back later and said they had nothing reported in that area and the guy probably wouldn't report because he was in restricted airspace and would be violated. The boys thought that the guys pants were probably violated for sure. They never heard anything further.

After landing from another low-level mission and parking, Sluggo's crew chief called him on interphone and asked him, "What did you run into sir?" When they went out to look there was a very large bloody dent in the leading edge of the right wing between an engine pod and the fuselage. It was rough that day at low-level and with all the turbulence they didn't feel anything. The only thing they could think of was they might have hit a condor or a pterodactyl, or a UFO, or so the boys mused, the BUFF wings are tough and thanks to St. Elmo it didn't hit the cockpit...score BUFF one, big ass unknown bird zero.

"Stinky Creek" was a road junction high in the Sierra National Forest, it consisted of a general store and saloon across from a park campground, a horse stable down the road and a hotel and restaurant up the road (it was also located below a route that the boys used for descending into home base). It was a tradition for the CFIC guys, and only the guys, to have a no holds barred camping and fishing stag weekend every year dubbed only "The Annual." It was not uncommon that the saloon would get buzzed by a BUFF or TIF a few times during the week

prior to the event...watch out, we're coming back. The locals looked forward to the Annual as much as the boys did, it was a must-see event. There are many stories from the Annuals, here's a couple.

It was tradition to conduct a different formal ceremony on the bridge over Stinky Creek every year. A wedding, marrying new guys into the unit, a divorce for old guys leaving the unit, even a graduation; three guys in full cap and gown were presented diplomas after completing Staff College...and other ceremonies

too terrible to mention, some on horseback, use your imagination. Sluggo returned from a day of fishing to find a horse in his tent, and yes, the horse left him a present.

The guys had an area of about 15 isolated campsites, complete with a palatial one-hole facility, that they would try to grab...the Rangers helped because they liked to keep the crew dogs together away from the rest of the campers. One year there was one spot left in the boys' area when a couple with two tween kids showed up with a fancy pop-up camper and took the remaining space. The guys warned them that that probably wasn't a good idea to park there as the night would be loud and boisterous and there were plenty of other empty spaces away from the boys. They said that that was OK and not a problem for them...well, that night was all it was cracked up to be. One of the very big guys, call sign "Slim" staggered into the john in the middle of the night and promptly took a nap. The wife was up at the crack of dawn and made her way to the facility...apparently Slim neglected to lock the door...she opened it and there he was, sound asleep in all his glory, with his pants around his ankles. According to eye witnesses the family did a record NASCAR pit stop and broke all land speed records exiting stage left.

Now back to the airdrome for some good pilot stuff, approaches and landings of assorted kinds. As previously mentioned CFIC had great rapport with ATC, if it was daytime, good weather and no traffic in the area, and especially in the winter (fewer tourists), the boys would declare visual flight rules (VFR) and request the "Scenic Letdown" from ATC, a wonderful tour of a famous National Park; but don't go too low, use good judgement, don't disturb the natives, and don't get caught. Back in the traffic pattern for about an hour and a half of missed approaches, multiple engine out approaches, flaps up, ground effect demonstrations, rudder/elevator out, touch and go landings (12 or so...the record was 17) and other stuff...things the ICs would need to know to teach a new crew dog old tricks.

One of the key demonstrations was to show how easy it was for a pilot to become distracted during approach and landings by unusual situations, be it weather, disturbances in the cockpit, emergencies, or other oddities... remember "Fly the Aircraft." One of Sluggo's favorite tricks was opening the BUFF side window while in the traffic pattern...this was unheard of and never done in flight, although not dangerous or prohibited. While the IC was distracted trying to figure what was happening, Sluggo would raise the landing gear. About 50% of the time the IC wouldn't notice until the aircraft was well into final approach that his wheels were up...remember "Fly the Aircraft."

One day an almond grower (pronounced "Am-und" in that neck of the woods) drove up to the base main gate with a big piece of metal in the back of his truck, he said, "I think this belongs to you guys." Turns out it was part of the flap from a CFIC tanker...the sky is falling.

The base nuclear Weapons Storage Area (WSA) was located several hundred yards east of the runway. One of the CFIC tankers got a little close on a practice engine out missed approach and set off all the WSA intrusion alarms (new and more sensitive ones had been recently installed). He reported back to the boys that it was great fun to watch all the Sky Cops thrashing around while responding. Well you can probably guess what was next, if you kicked in right rudder on a touch and go and skid towards the WSA, off would go the alarms. After a few similar episodes, the edict came down from on high, "There will be no more intentional maneuvers designed to set off the WSA alarm systems...do you copy?" Sluggo thought, "but that was great training for the Sky Cops."

One day Sluggo was descending into the local area in one of the older BUFFs, when he put the gear down, his number one hydraulic light came on indicating failure of that pack, (located in the landing gear well, powering one set of wheels, steering, and brakes) not a big deal as there was plenty of backup including standby pumps. Alas, no touch and go landings today only low approaches. When it was time for a full stop the procedure was to stop straight ahead on the runway, so maintenance could switch a crossover valve, allowing the jet to taxi off. The landing was uneventful...when the crew chief plugged into interphone Sluggo informed him that he had lost the number one hydraulic pack, the crew chief informed Sluggo that was indeed true as the pack was gone. The crew shut down and looked up into the wheel well and sure enough the pack wasn't there, it must have fallen out during the descent and was probably camping somewhere in the high Sierras. "This BUFF is beat and wants to retire" thought Sluggo.

One more traffic pattern story. One of the CFIC guys was circling to land when he hit a large flock of ducks, suspecting engine damage, he put the jet on the ground, upon inspection there was a perfectly plucked mallard stuck between the drop tank and the wing...duck for dinner anyone?

At long last, Sluggo pinned on the gold leaves of a Major...the lame excuse, "but I'm only a dumb Captain" won't work anymore, so let's try "but I'm a brand-new Major." One day at the weekly all hands meeting, the chief, "Lucky" notified the troops that CFIC had been designated as a SAC elite academic organization. "Great," he said, "now the bad news, we must conform to a myriad of new requirements and we will be inspected for compliance." Inspection is one of the most despised words in the crew dog dictionary.

Soon the edict came down from mother SAC that all such organizations will be 'ISD' compliant post-haste. Everyone asked what the hell is an ISD. "Well it's *Instructional Systems Design* and it's the entire process of analysis of learning needs and goals and the development of a delivery system to meet those needs," said Lucky reading from the SAC edict and trying to act smart. "Sluggo, you and "Plato" (call sign of a fellow CFIC IP of Greek heritage and former BUFF school house instructor) are hereby appointed as the CFIC ISD officers...make it happen." After meeting with the school house guys and extensive research, Plato and Sluggo came up with a plan…get lots of fancy audio-visual education stuff, TVs, VCRs, video cameras, slide projectors, etc., put them in a room called a "Learning Center," with educational furniture, and an AV library with as much aviation media as we can get our hands…"if you build it they will come." But who will pay?

The boys discovered that they were covered by a SAC Authorization Code to get a ton of AV type stuff that was depot funded…and so they did with the help of some little old ladies with green eye shades in supply. As they were looking through all the gear that they could order, they saw within their authorization category with all the rest of the stuff, they could order a Mobile Telemetry Station, so they ordered one just for grins never thinking it would be approved by SAC…but it was. "What are we going to do with that?" they mused. "Well we could put it in our parking lot…but perhaps we should cancel that order, before we get nailed, that's a good idea, let's do it, color it gone…no harm no foul." The Learning Center was a huge success, the troops actually used and liked it, and it garnered high praise during a SAC inspection. Plato and Sluggo also authored a 250-page B-52 Flight Instructor Guide which was a best seller throughout the command. Even blind pigs can find some acorns every once in a while.

The Wing was in transition; the BUFFs assigned to the base consisted of B-52 "Tall Tail" model E's and F's which were the only ones left in SAC that had been used only for training, the B-52 D models which had been used for ARC Light training, and some B-52 Cs. These aircraft were all being moved to other bases and the newest B-52 G and H models would assume the SAC BUFF training mission. The G and H models were so much different than the Tall Tails that they could almost be called B-53s.

The H model was awesome with eight TF-33 fan jets often referred to as your "eight good buddies"... power galore and no dreaded water injection...what a machine. The B-52 H continues to fly today and will aviate well into the foreseeable future.

But wait, what do I see on the flight line...could it be a "Crested Dove?" Crested Dove was the code word for a SAC operation that was initiated during the height of the cold war in the early 70's. 60 some odd obsolete B-52 models scattered throughout many SAC bases were about to be retired as they were the oldest BUFFs around, made in the 50's and had not been upgraded with any of the current modifications. Some big brains had an idea. "Why don't we start up and taxi these ancient grounded beasts around the ramp to different parking spots every few weeks and we can really fool the Russians as their satellites snap away" ...and so it began.

At some point after spending some $10 million, some other big brain thought, who are we trying to kid everybody knows these old BUFFs aren't combat ready...we need to send them to the scrap heap as these tragic BUFFs hadn't flown in years. The new CFIC chief, call sign "Weeble" called Sluggo and Plato into his office and uttered the famous words, "I've got some good news and some bad news. The good news is,

you're going down to sunny Arizona for a few days, and you're going to fly down there in your very own B-52 for which you will sign a hand receipt and assume ownership. The bad news is it's a C model and its last flight was around three years ago, and by the way, you must do it at 185 kts. with the flaps and landing gear down. (The maximum airspeed for flaps down was 190 kts.... don't exceed it or they might fall off). The maintenance toads inform us that if you raise the landing gear and flaps, they may not come back down and that would be very bad … the jet would be very hard to land with no wheels or flaps and you also wouldn't be able to fly around forever because we don't know if the air refueling system would work either."

So Sluggo, Plato and a CFIC NAV call sign "Poo Bear" (minimum B 52 crew two pilots and a NAV) set out to take the inglorious C model to its final resting place, the joint Service Military Aircraft Storage and Disposition Center (MASDC), better known as the "Bone Yard". The wrench benders worked like dogs to get the C ready to fly, all the engines worked, necessary systems looked OK, ejection seats and parachutes were checked, and all extraneous equipment of any future use was removed. The maintainers briefed the guys "the flaps will be disabled in the full down position with the circuit breakers pulled, and the landing gear will be pinned for ground operations and cannot be raised."

The fateful day arrived, pre-flight was normal, all the motors started and as they taxied out the tower cleared them for takeoff with a "good luck Buffy 52," (their call sign). Takeoff roll was great, as they didn't have a full load of gas and the motors worked fine. As they were climbing out at 185 kts, ATC called Buffy 52, and asked them if they were experiencing any problems because of the slow climb out airspeed. Sluggo said "no, that's just as fast as this old girl can go." They climbed to 20,000 feet, the pressurization worked. Poo Bear the NAV came upstairs for the ride as most of the navigation and radar gear had been removed from the basement. The trip was uneventful, upon arrival Sluggo requested a 360-degree overhead pattern (typically used by fighter aircraft) so the old girl could look good on her last landing.

After touchdown, (the brakes worked) the tower directed Buffy 52 to the follow-me truck and through the elephant graveyard they taxied to their parking spot. They shut Buffy 52 down and deplaned. They were met by a

Navy Lieutenant, (remember the boneyard was a joint Service operation), who saluted smartly and said, "please sign this hand receipt on the dotted line Sir, and I'll take ownership of the aircraft as the representative of MASDC." "This little ceremony is very sad" thought Sluggo, "and to add insult to injury I have to turn this old bird over to a Navy Squid who's going to turn her into beer cans." So, the boys cheated death again, toasted Buffy 52 with a few beers that night, and caught a tanker home the next day.

Sluggo detected a disturbance in the "Force" and that never bodes well for crew dogs. The base personnel people informed Sluggo that he was required to call the SAC flesh peddlers (assignment folks) post haste, he knew that nothing good could come from that, he also knew

he was due for a reassignment. So here we go, from the best BUFF flying job in the world (Sluggo was now the CFIC Bomber Branch Chief) to who knows what. Sluggo talked to the dreaded assignment dudes and was informed that he was going to Headquarters, United States Air Force, Directorate of Operations, The Pentagon, Washington, D.C. Sluggo had never been there and had never been assigned East of the Mississippi. Sluggo asked, "Do they have any airplanes there?" ...the answer came back, "No just desks, and by the way, it's a "by name" request—somebody senior thinks you will be perfect for the job." "Who requested me?" asked Sluggo thinking how he'd like to get his hands on whoever. "We don't release that information" was the answer. Sluggo said "I really don't want to stop flying, maybe I'll put my papers in, get out and go with the airlines." The answer was, "That bluff won't work with us, we've heard it many times before and since Vietnam is over, we've got plenty of pilots, go ahead." "Perhaps I've been a bit hasty" replied Sluggo, "I guess you called my buff and I'm off to the Puzzle Palace." And so, the die was cast, he was soon to become an aviation "static display." Sluggo flew his last BUFF mission, went to a great going away party in his honor, was presented his B-52 5,000-hour pin, packed his bags, and headed East on a new adventure. Will Sluggo ever again fly his beloved BUFF again...I wonder?

Chapter Eighteen: Pentagon – "The Puzzle Palace, and How Sluggo Learned to Become a Staff Weenie"

Sluggo has many stories about his stay at the Pentagon…here's a few. And so it came to pass, Major Sluggo was off to our Nation's Capital…or at least to a place in Virginia across the Potomac from it. He sold his beloved MG and his equally beloved Toyota Land Cruiser and associated tear drop camping trailer, both bright red (trailer now quite in vogue I might add), none of which were practical for a cross country jaunt and neither of which he assumed would be DC friendly. He bought a new Toyota Celica, nice car but…oh well, packed it up and took off in a cloud of San Jaquan Valley dust. Took I-80, first stop Winnemucca, Nevada…a garden spot famous for a Red-Light District and the Buckaroo Hall of Fame. "I'll have neither," said Sluggo "but maybe a few games of chance before I retire for the night." As the saying goes, "The house always wins," and it did, he quickly reached his limit and quit. "That wasn't much fun" he declared. "I'd rather be flying" he thought as he made his way across the U.S. finally arriving in Virginia, checked into a motel, full stop and amen, "That was a long trip, almost as much fun as a 24-hour BUFF mission."

Sluggo was being assigned to the AF XO, Directorate of Operations run by a 3-Star General with a palatial office on the E ring 4th floor where all the big boys lived, and yes windows…but not so fast, you're really being assigned to XOOOE, AF Exercise Branch run by a Lieutenant Colonel and deep in the bowels of the Pentagon basement…more about the basement later. He had a Major as a sponsor but when he tried to contact him, he was informed that he was on an extended temporary duty (TDY) and wouldn't be back for several months. "I don't need no stinking sponsor," thought Sluggo, "I can handle this by myself and I've got a few days before I sign in so let's find a place to live. With two Air Force Bases in the area I should have no problem staying at one or the other until I find a place to call home." Checking into the BOQ office at Bolling AFB, Sluggo asked if he could bunk down there

for a few weeks, the clerk said "Not a problem sir, let me see your orders." He complied and after the clerk looked at them he said, "You're assigned to the Pentagon, not Bolling, I am sorry but you can stay here for a day or two and then check in every day to see if we have any rooms." Sluggo was shocked so he made his way to Andrews AFB and got the same story only worse…one day then day to day, "I guess I'm not in the real Air Force anymore" he bemoaned.

Sluggo called his new office and talked to his deputy boss about housing who said, "There's an apartment complex down the highway close to the Pentagon that rents furnished flats month to month, you should try them," and he did. After checking in with a one-month lease, Sluggo thought, "this should work for a while – it's a quick drive to the Pentagon but it's not cheap, I need to find something more permanent and not so rich." While checking out the neighborhood, he noticed a sign in a small strip mall across the street, *Scooter's Saloon, Delectables and Cure-alls…Grand Opening*. Sluggo stopped in for a cold one and liked what he saw good food, good beer, and lots of folks who looked like him with short haircuts, no doubt a military hangout…more about Scooter's later.

The area was filled with apartment complexes, it was often called *Washington's Bedroom*, and so he began the search for a new abode. There was also a little Army Post, called Cameron Station two blocks away with a Commissary and Exchange… "all the comforts of home, I think I'll stay here…life is good." At the end of the month, Sluggo moved into a studio apartment on the 10th floor of a fairly new "no kids" building a few blocks up the street from Scooters. He rented some furniture and settled in; his balcony looked down on what he thought was a school…but turned out to be a juvenile detention facility…good place to watch the excitement during the occasional escape attempts. The entire time he lived there, he kept looking for his bedroom and never found it… it's a studio apartment with only one room you bozo. So off to work we go to become a Pentagon staff weenie.

The Pentagon, the five-sided puzzle palace…what a place. Now a few factoids. The Pentagon building spans 28.7 acres and includes an

additional 5.1 acres as a central courtyard, often called Ground Zero, a presumed target for Russian ICBMs. There is also a Concourse on the southeast side of the second floor of the building, which contains

a mini-shopping mall. It's one of the biggest office buildings in the world, working space for about 25,000 military and civilians and 17 miles of corridors. They say it's possible for a person to walk between any two points in the Pentagon in less than seven minutes…sure, you bet. Part of orientation to the building includes a handy guide to help you get around. It's a little long, but after reading one can see the why it's called the Puzzle Palace, so take a deep breath and read.

"The concentric rings are designated from the center out as "A" through "E" (with an additional "F" and "G" in the basement). "E" Ring offices are the only ones with outside views (generally occupied by the Stars and heavy breather civilians). Office numbers go clockwise around each of the rings and have two parts: a nearest-corridor number (1 to 10) followed by a bay number (00 to 99), so office numbers range from 100 to 1099. These corridors radiate out from the central

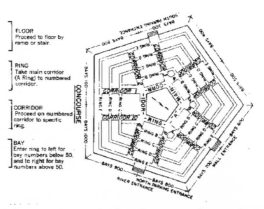

courtyard, with corridor 1 beginning with the Concourse's south end. Each numbered radial corridor intersects with the corresponding numbered group of offices (for example, corridor 5 divides the 500-series office block)."

"Floors in the Pentagon are lettered "B" for Basement and "M" for Mezzanine, both of which are below ground level. Above ground floors are numbered 1 to 5. Room numbers are given as the floor, concentric ring, and office number (which is in turn the nearest corridor number followed by the bay number). Thus, office 2B315 is on the second floor, B ring, and nearest to corridor 3 (between corridors 2 and 3). One way to get to this office would be to go to the second floor, get to the A (innermost) ring, go to and take corridor 3, and then turn left on ring B to get to bay 15."

You got all that? This chart shows only one level…there's seven more!

Sluggo reported into his new office in BD927, the XOOOE Exercise Branch, the office in charge of Air Force participation in the Joint Chiefs of Staff (JCS) Military Exercise Program. "Right up my alley," thought Sluggo, "not only do I know very little about the JCS, I know nothing about their exercise program…start drinking from the old firehose." The office was attached to the AF Command Center, impressive two-story room with large viewing screens and a command  balcony for the big boys. Also attached was the AF Operations Center manned 24/7 to monitor the entire AF and all the generals misbehaving. Sluggo's office was a small cubbyhole with two Action Officers (AO's)…aka gophers, a Lt Col Chief, (C-130 trash hauler pilot), Major Sluggo and two administrative NCO's.

The Basement was a wild place that didn't quite conform to the above ground organized lay out. Many strange hallways, loading docks, doorways with combination locks and only a number, no name, forklifts zooming around, pipes and wires everywhere in the ceiling, not a beautiful place. Located in one hallway was a bright purple water fountain...no one could say why it was purple...it became the North Star of the AF basement...the central locator. "Go to the purple water fountain, proceed down

that hallway, take a right two corridors down, the left at the next small hallway, the office that you're looking for is three doors on the right by the sign that says F Ring, but it's really not F Ring. If that isn't the office that you're looking for...go back to the purple water fountain and try again." One Monday when the basement dwellers came to work, the purple water fountain was gone (this was after Sluggo's time). Conspiracy theories ran rampant, who stole it and where was it, the outrage went on for several months until it was discovered in a maintenance shop...it was due to be replaced with a modern fixture. It was rescued and became a permanent shrine to the basement encased in glass complete with a plaque stating its history...it's still there.

In one basement hallway there was a big sign "Caution, Deaf Workers, Hearing Protection Required" the Defense Printing Plant was down the way and extremely loud. Defense hired deaf employees to work in the noisiest parts. There were critters that lived in the basement, mostly rodents although cats or other things were spotted several times, one office claimed that a rat named Sea Biscuit raced through the office about 10 am every morning. Broken pipes were a common occurrence, both water and other disgusting stuff.

Since the Pentagon was built on swampland, it was constantly sinking into the muck, one fix was to drill a hole in the basement floor and pump in cement. During one such episode the pumpers goofed; punctured a main sewer pipe and filled it full of cement. In came the Bobcats to dig down and fix the problem resulting in some great smells and a huge pile of dirt in a main hallway. The pile was soon decorated with many home-made signs and tombstones, "Bury Dead Rats Here," "We Gotta Get Out of this Place," "Army Sucks," "Kilroy Wasn't Here," "Navy Sucks More," "Tomb of the Unknown Action Officer," you get the idea. Contrary to popular expectations, there was no top-secret bomb proof hideout under the Pentagon...only swampland and dirt.

Sluggo's job was to coordinate the AF participation in the worldwide JCS command post exercises from cradle to grave. This included coordinating the scenarios, determining participation, timing, operations, running and training the battle staff, exercise play, after action reports, etc. throughout the Air Staff. Since there was no war going on, these were big deals with actual play up to the 4-star level. Lots of face time running through the building, and lots of opportunities to screw up briefing the heavies and holding their hands during the exercises.

As the months went by, Sluggo became rather proficient at the job. One morning, his boss came in and announced that the office was expanding and getting a new AO, he turned out to be another B-52 driver call sign "Buck" a really good, slightly wild guy that Sluggo had known from his Arc Light days on Guam and Thailand. "This could be real trouble with the two BUFFers in the same office," thought Sluggo…and that did come to pass in spades. Buck settled in and they became a team.

One afternoon with their boss they attended an exercise in the National Military Command Center (NMCC) with the Service 4-star Generals and Admirals in attendance. During their deliberations there was a Marine Corps Major flitting around the head table with briefing papers for the 4-stars. Sluggo asked, "Who is that guy…seems like he's telling the big boys what to do?" His boss replied, "He just made LtCol, is on the fast track in JCS, and rumor has it that he will soon be transferring to the White House." "He seems a bit pompous around all those heavies," thought Sluggo, "but if he's going to the White House, I don't think I'll ever have the displeasure to cross his path." Will Sluggo meet him in the future…I wonder.

Sluggo and Buck became fast friends. As they ambled through the halls of power, they picked up the handle "Bobbsey Twins." Buck lived only a couple of blocks away from Sluggo in a high-rise condo, so they decided to carpool to work. With four riders they could use the high occupancy vehicle (HOV) lanes so they would buzz by bus stops to pick up two more riders going their way to be legal. (In the future this was to become what Pentagon and DC folk lore called "Slugging," people standing on certain corners in "Slug Lines" depending on their destination waiting to get picked up). Soon they formed a real carpool with two other Pentagonites who lived near…as an extra benefit, they could also park in the close-in four-member carpool rows in North Parking which was great especially if the weather sucked. Naturally, since they lived so close to each other Scooter's Saloon became a mandatory post work destination.

There was an unwritten rule...no wearing of uniforms after 7pm...so go home and change if you want to come back...this was a good check on overdoing it, especially on TGIF.

Many Scooter stories abound, here's a couple. The Scooter crowd was a diverse collection of youngish military and civilian inside the beltway folks, all services, all career fields, active duty and retired, from two-star generals on down, including a notorious SEAL, Red Cell anyone? Romances and breakups, happiness and agony, fights and hugs, 10 K's and charity golf tournaments, and everything in between. It was truly the "Cheers" of Alexandria, Virginia before "Cheers" was born. There was a huge bay window on one end of the bar looking out on the parking lot, it was called the "magic window of life" exposing everything and anything that went on in the parking lot...free entertainment, enough said.

One TGIF night, two former Army guys were starting to get into it, alcohol was a factor...one was Special Forces (SF); the other a Huey pilot who had lost part of his foot when his helicopter was shot up in Vietnam...he wore a special shoe. When it got physical the chopper guy took a swing at the SF guy and the scuffle began. During the melee, the helo driver's special shoe fell off and the SF guy grabbed it, ran outside, and threw it on the roof of the bar. To make a long story short, the shoe was retrieved, with apologies. "I didn't know that part of your foot was in there" said the SF guy, then peace was declared, and drunken hugs of mutual love prevailed.

A Marine Corps Major, a Scooter regular, had an ongoing affair with comely Scooter regular female flight attendant... (she categorized her job description as "Aisle Whore") ...they were quite an item. On the night of the annual Marine Corps Ball...a really big deal, full mess uniform and all the trimmings, as any Marine can attest...our Major had the stones to show up at Scooters after the ball with another woman...and the "Aisle Whore" was at the other end of the bar. Well, the shit hit the fan along with a very large Irish Coffee that was thrown in the face and all over the dress uniform of one Marine 0-4 ... beguiled female one, USMC zero. Enough Scooter stories, but for now...back to the Pentagon.

Sluggo and Buck noticed a slow change in the force, the Russian Bear threat was receding, and the regional contingency threat was growing and the JCS exercise program was slowly adapting. One day their boss said he was moving on to a new assignment and the Bobbsey Twins would run the shop, they had both pinned on Lt Col leaves by this time. As the days passed, they hired a young Major ex-Jolly Green Giant helicopter pilot, call sign "Ruff." He was a big gangly Texan and when he watched the boys in action, he would just shake his head. "How will I learn this stuff; they didn't teach this in Squadron Officer School," he mused. Sluggo said, "Just sit back and watch, it will eventually come." Ruff was a real piece of work, one day he declared that he was going to run the Marine Corps Marathon… with little or no training…he finished but screwed up his feet with blisters and shin splints so bad he went on sick leave for a week. Sluggo's big boss (not a runner) was really pissed as the office was quite busy. He eventually cooled down and life was good again and Sluggo told Ruff to maintain a low profile around the front office…in fact, avoid it. Ruff was always a joy and it soon became the Bobbsey Twins and Ruff the Duff prowling the Air Staff halls.

The guys 3-star chief felt the need to gain visibility on operations with the Air Force Secretary and his civilian staff so to that end he proposed a series of ops-oriented briefings. Since it was the 10th anniversary of the North Vietnam bombing campaign, Linebacker II, he suggested flying in a couple of B-52 guys to do the brief. The 2-star said "I've got the Bobbsey Twins in the basement they're BUFF drivers and I know they both flew in Linebacker. We'll put them in flight suits and let them brief the Secretary.

And so, it came to pass with many dry runs, fits and starts, and professionally produced slides (this was of course before the day of Power Point). The briefing went exceptionally well. After the event the Secretary congratulated them and asked them, "Where did you guys fly in from." Without thinking Buck responded, "We flew in from the basement, sir." The General's jaw dropped but the Secretary had a hearty laugh and said, "Great to have guys like you in the building." The General smiled indicating all was well…this was the first of many various "Flight Suit Briefings" to the senior staff.

One of the young NCOs in the office asked the boys if they liked lobsters as his brother ran a fishing boat Up East and could fly the critters into National Airport. So, they ordered a batch and the plan went seamless and the live lobsters were great. They asked the kid, "how many can your bro get" and the answer was, "how many do you want?"

And so it began and soon they were getting weekly orders from a raft of people all over the building, this is getting out of control thought the boys, so they subcontracted the work out to various agents in other offices. The deal was legit as they did the deed on their lunch hour, no government assets were used, they were  flown in commercially, and they sold them at cost, their work was pro bono – their compensation only getting free lobster meat with each batch.

A couple of lobster stories. The boys' two-star General boss asked them to order some big lobsters as his three-star boss was coming over for dinner…so they did, and all went well. A couple of weeks later the three star was having the two star over for dinner and he ordered some lobsters with the stipulation that they had to be bigger than the ones they got for the two star…and they were considerably.

One of the Colonel's down the hall stopped by and asked the guys what was the biggest lobster they could get. He said that one of his buddies was a veterinarian and every time he went over to his place for dinner, he would greet him with some weird exotic animal. They talked to their fisherman and he said, "I've got a 25 pounder and a couple of smaller ones around 20 lbs. in the tank." They passed it on to the Colonel and he said, "get me the big one." And so, it came to pass, the big boy arrived in his own shipping box, his claws were as big as footballs. The Colonel prepositioned the lobster in his pantry and when the vet arrived they went out to his kitchen to get a drink and the Colonel

STRATEGIC SEAFOOD — Free enterprise, the Reagan administration's ultimate weapon in the war on America's current economic ills, has caught on at the Pentagon.

Deep in the bowels of DoD headquarters, two stalwart souls with an eye for an untapped market and a fast buck are running a lobster ring. The operation, conducted out of a computer room tied into the World Wide Military Command and Control early warning defense system (WWMCCS), handles about 350 fresh Maine lobsters a week and, according to one of the partners, business has been brisk.

Every Thursday, DoD workers trek down to meet their crustacean connection and pay $4 each in advance for lobsters weighing on average about one and a quarter pounds. Fridays the creatures are delivered, "alive and kicking," to satisfied customers from throughout the building.

Three hundred fifty lobsters of that size equal almost a quarter ton a week. It's reassuring to know that if the enemy somehow gets through the WWMCCS system with a sneak attack, this second line of defense stands — or more precisely, crawls — ready to fight them back.

FEDERAL TIMES, AUGUST 31, 1981

led the monster out on a leash…win one for the Colonel and the vet ate exotic crow…and a great time was had by all. The Colonel said he had to borrow a huge pan from a mess hall that covered all the burners of his stove and had a hell of a time getting the creature in the pot and cooked, as it took an hour to get the water to boil. He reported mission accomplished and that the meat was sweet and good.

As you can see by the Federal Times article, soon the lobster operation got out to the real world and the game was up; actually, the boys were ready to declare a going out of business sale as it was becoming a big pain…it was great fun, but it was just one of those things. The boys came out fine, no harm, no *fowl* (only claws), and some great dinners.

Christmas time in the Pentagon was a real hoot and a great excuse for parties and more parties. It became a real challenge to see what Air Staff office could have the greatest event in terms of originality, food, booze, and wild craziness. Of course, there was every theme you could think of, lots of Santa and elves, reindeers, snowmen and snow queens, and other characters, you get the idea. One office hired an actor, a spitting image of President Reagan who made the rounds and posed for pictures…he even sounded like him. Another office had a large roasted pig complete with apple in mouth as an eatable centerpiece. Flyers were distributed throughout the building advertising time and place. Several folks put out a rating pamphlet giving the previous year's parties scores from one to five on eats, spirits and ambiance.

The basement fighter jocks down the hall from the boys' office were planning a blast to end all blasts (and it almost did), including keg beer and a Mrs. Santa Claus stripper on a large stage constructed of their desks

 pushed together. One of them knew that Buck had a relative who was a beer distributor in Maryland and asked if he could supply a few kegs, when the answer was "Yes," "How many do you need?" was the question. "How about three…no make that four…can he deliver to the Pentagon North Loading Dock" (the North Loading Dock was also the lobster point of entry). And so, it came to pass, the stripper was having so much fun she invited a few of her stripper pals over to join the action. The party was a roaring success with lines of girls and guys in the hall, waiting to get in, after the event red beer cups littered the basement halls and

stairways, and yes, all the beer was consumed. As you can see, the party made the press. In the aftermath, a few of the fighter mafia organizers got their hands slapped but since there were also senior folks in attendance the punishment was only a few demerits. Buck was not reprimanded as he only supplied the beer. This was before the deglamorization of alcohol in the military and well before and considerably tamer than the Tail Hook debacle, but the wild and crazy days of Pentagon Christmas bashes and wild parties in the military were slowly coming to a close…alas.

As was previously hinted the threat of the USSR red peril was on the wane and regional contingencies and terrorism were emerging as the threat du jour. Sluggo and the XOOOE guys picked up more missions and people, in addition to exercises they became responsible for the management and training of the AF battle staff, and the AF Joint Exercise budget including the large airlift slice. State sponsored terrorism in the middle east was rapidly bubbling up as were other contingencies like the Titan Missile crisis, Iran hostage taking, Beirut and other bombings, aircraft hijacking, attacks against U.S. GIs worldwide, Grenada rescue, and others. New U.S. military response included formation of the Joint Special Operations Command (JSOC) hush hush, the highly mobile Rapid Deployment Joint Task Force, (soon to be USCENTCOM), and other JCS initiatives all including Joint Exercises.

As a result, the guys were deeply involved in all the joint planning and execution…things were busy. To make matters worse, Buck was informed that he was a year short of making his flying gates (he was a

Topless dancer has AF officers in hot water

WASHINGTON (AP) — The Air Force has disciplined several officers for hiring a topless dancer to perform at a pre-Christmas party in the Pentagon, a spokesman said Wednesday.

Capt. John Whitaker, the spokesman, said "appropriate action" had been taken against the officers, but he declined to go into detail because of what he said were restrictions under the federal Privacy Act.

"There was a party in the tactical division of the deputy chief of staff for plans and operations in the Pentagon basement," Whitaker said. "The dancer was paid for out of personal funds."

The officers, including fighter pilots now on staff duty, drew the ire of the Air Force officials because the action violated Air Force policy against "practices that are not in good taste and that are offensive to the Air Force," Whitaker said.

maintenance officer prior to going to pilot training), so he was off to Andrews for a couple of years to fly T-39's, the AF corporate jet. To keep his 2-star boss informed, Sluggo put together several papers summarizing the situations, offering some suggestions, and even some predicting where some future trouble spots might pop up. Never thinking that they would go any farther than his immediate boss, he was quite surprised when some made it as far as the 4-star level including the AF Chief of Staff (his boss had sent them upstairs). Subsequently Sluggo was called into the 2-star's office and informed that he was being directed by the 3-star XO to put together a Contingency Support and Anti-terrorism Center in the basement since there was currently no function on the Air Staff that was satisfying that new requirement. He said Sluggo's guys seemed to be the most logical choice since they were already involved in the Joint arena and had advised him during recent exercises and seemed to know what to do. Sluggo was also told within reason, not to be constrained by space, personnel or funding, and by the way, we needed it yesterday.

There was a large computer room with a raised floor behind the command center that housed a huge server during Vietnam now occupied by odds and ends. The boys took it over and Sluggo began to hire; fighter guys (one later became a 4-star…must have been Sluggo's expert training), airlifters, special operators, bomber drivers including two from Sluggo's old CFIC BUFF unit, tanker toads, search and rescue, admin folks, bean counters, a detailed intelligence body and a sky cop. With all those people, communication in the big room included a lot of yelling…they needed a computer system of some sorts. When asked, they were told that the Air Staff LAN would be available in a year or so. Sluggo said, "We can't wait that long, so we'll buy our own local system." That got approved and soon there was a sparkling new Wang unit on everyone's desk. Remember, they were in an old computer room, so they ran all the cables under the floor to a large closet that housed the server (it was very loud) and with a giant 10-pound memory disc, somewhere around 200 MBs.

Well, it was quite cold under the floor due to the air conditioning, someone thought what a great place to store beer and so they did…by the case. Soon other folks heard about it and it became the basement cold beer depository for several offices. Sluggo also ordered modular furniture for the gang, 20 plus positions. One day it arrived at the loading dock and soon the hall was lined with scores of boxes…some assembly required? Professional assembly came with the furniture for a modest cost, GSA said we don't need no stinking assemblers, we can do it…well you guessed it when they saw the million boxes they said, "We can't possibly put that together." So, the gang tackled it themselves, "this can't be that hard." Late nights after work and on the weekend. Not an easy task with right and left and center pieces, drawers, cabinets, huge sacks of hardware, nuts and bolts, and so on. Well, they did it although it was never completely right, with stuff left over, but it worked and looked great. Sluggo had a cubicle with a direct phone line to the 3-star's office, which he never used...but the General did. When the smoke cleared, the office totaled 19 Air Staffers plus Sluggo. He thought, "When I leave this my slot will go to a Colonel, no way they'll let a Lt Col run this empire."

You might recall from an earlier chapter the question was asked, "Will Sluggo ever again fly his beloved BUFF again" ...well, here's the answer. Sluggo heard through the Pentagon grapevine that his new 3-star boss, the Director of Operations (XO), a fighter pilot of the nth degree wanted to add to his credentials and go fly the BUFF. He also heard that the general was scheduled (by his non-BUFF Exec) to go to the B-52 training base and fly with a student crew. Sluggo went to his 2-star and said, "Not trying to butt in, but the XO should fly with my old unit CFIC, the "Top Gun" guys, they would really show him what the jet can do." A week later, his boss called him in and said, "That was a great suggestion Sluggo and by the way, you're going with him."

And so, it came to pass, he called his old CFIC buddies and gave them the word. The schedule was set, a little ground training, several simulator rides and a flight with the CFIC Bomber Chief, call sign "Greek" ...the chap that replaced Sluggo when he left. Sluggo departed with the general in his sleek little T-39 executive jet, one stop for gas at Offutt AFB (Sluggo's projected next home) then off to B-52 land. They arrived, next a series of ground training, simulators, mission planning, with Sluggo assisting at all events; next stop BUFF aviation. They were flying a B-52 H (the model with the big motors, "your eight good buddies").

The mission was the regular CFIC profile; takeoff, air refueling, low level route, then back for lots of pattern and landing work. Greek flew in the copilot's seat with the general in the pilot's seat. The general had his hands full with air refueling but he did have several unaided contacts. Coming up on the end of the track, Greek put Sluggo in the seat and thankfully his refueling talents were still there. He remained in the seat with the general for low-level, flying a route (low and fast) that he had flown countless times. Climbing out of low level and since it was a H model BUFF and the airplane was light fuel wise, Sluggo firewalled it and demonstrated a max performance climb and the BUFF flew like a rocket. The general said, "OK Sluggo, I'm impressed, level this beast off I must pee." Back home, numerous landings were had by all and the general planted the jet firmly a few times. After the flight, the general was full of praise and accolades. "This airplane is a lot harder to fly than I thought it would be…and it's impressive." On the official flight records, Greek put a notation next to Sluggo's name that went something like this, "Do not ever allow this individual near an airplane again." Alas, that was to come true, as Sluggo never flew his beloved BUFF again.

Time marches on, terrorism was becoming a growth industry, the office was busy and Sluggo was due to rotate to a new assignment. The orders came down "You have a by name request to go to Strategic Air Command Headquarters, Operations Directorate, Omaha Nebraska." Sluggo wanted to go back to flying BUFFs but it didn't appear that that was going to happen. He flew out to Omaha, found a nice apartment and put a deposit down on it, came back to DC and prepared to move. He had great going away parties at the Pentagon and at Scooters…" I'll miss them both." About a week before he was due to leave, he got a call from a very powerful Colonel soon to be General, in the 3-star's office who asked "You don't really want to go back to SAC as a staff puke do you? "Sluggo asked "What do you have in mind sir?" "We have the requirement to furnish a Colonel or Lt Col for a temporary assignment at the White House to serve on the staff of the soon to be formed Vice President's Task Force on Combatting Terrorism… and you would be perfect." Sluggo thought about a second and asked, "When do I start?" The Colonel said "I'll go to the 3-star for his blessing, I should know within a week or so." Sluggo said "I need to know sooner as my movers are coming in a day." The Colonel called him back and said, "Cancel your movers." So Sluggo did, went down to Scooters and said "Thanks for the party but I'm staying," lost his deposit on the apartment in Omaha, and prepared for a new adventure in the stratosphere…and we don't mean flying.

Chapter Nineteen: White House – "Terrorists Beware...You Can Run, But You Can't Hide"

In this Chronicle you will see references to National Security Decision Directives (NSDDs). These action documents tasked Executive Branch Departments and Agencies, defined official policy guidance and were all signed by the President. They were usually classified from Confidential through Top Secret. The NSDDs cited in this Chronicle have been declassified over the years and copies are available for reference online, just Google them if interested.

Sluggo's orders were changed and he was on his way to the White House as a member of the Working Group for the soon to be formed Task Force on Combating Terrorism chaired by Vice President George H. W. Bush. But what was this all about and why was this action being taken by the White House?

Serious words from Sluggo... he can be serious at times. Terrorism in some form has been around as long as man, although its definition has constantly been redefined over the ages, but when it happens you'll know it... "I believe that's terrorism." The kidnapping and murder of 11 Israeli athletics at the 1972 Olympics in Munich was a watershed event bringing the reality of international terrorism to the U.S. public through the media. Munich demonstrated for one of the first times very visibly an organized terror group, armed hostage taking as a tactic, and willingness for mass casualties and suicide. The U.S. Government reacted by forming several working groups during the next two administrations. Very little of substance was accomplished, just lots of meetings, as the general opinion was "it's a European and Middle East problem."

Usher in the 80's. The 1980's saw a dramatic increase of international terrorism including State sponsorship and multiple incidents directed specifically at the U.S. This isn't a complete review of all terrorism in the early 80's but it outlines certain very significant events that spawned the creation of the Vice President's Task Force on Combatting Terrorism.

- 1983, Beirut Lebanon, suicide bombing U.S. Embassy, 63 killed including 17 Americans.

- 1983, Beirut Lebanon, suicide bombing U.S. Marine Corps Barracks Compound, 217 U.S. Service personnel killed.

- 1984, Mediterranean Sea, Italian cruise ship *Achille Lauro* hijacked, crippled Jewish American civilian murdered, thrown overboard in his wheelchair to his death.

- 1985, Middle East, Trans World Airlines Flight 847 departing Athens hijacked in midair, rotated between Beirut and Algiers airports for the next three days trading hostages for fuel. A U.S. Navy diver on board was executed in Beirut, his body thrown out of the aircraft onto the tarmac. Remaining hostages eventually deplaned and held captive in Lebanon for the next two weeks.

TWA 847 hijacking was the crowning blow, (the straw that broke the camel's back…groan) as the ordeal was broadcast live into American homes on CNN with the vivid, never forget, pictures of the hijacker

holding a gun to the pilot's head. After 16 days through the direct intervention of President Reagan, the last hostages were finally released. Sluggo and his XOOOE Pentagon team activated on day one, 24/7 to support the military actions; it was a very intense response and highly covert…when the dust settled, the crew was awarded the Air Force Achievement Medal for "working highly sensitive and complex issues for the Joint Chiefs of Staff Crisis Action Team during a period of increased National tension." Because of the growing terrorism threat, NSDD 179 was signed in July 1985 which spawned the Task Force on Combatting Terrorism.

NSDD 179 ~ TASK FORCE ON COMBATTING TERRORISM

"International terrorism poses an increasing threat to U.S. citizens and our interests....to ensure that all appropriate resources of the United States Government are dedicated to this task, the Vice President is appointed to convene a government-wide task force on combatting terrorism. The Vice President will appoint a senior Executive Director...who may task any government Department or Agency, individual or organization to contribute to the work of the Task Force. To support the work of the Task Force, a working group will be established...the working group will prepare substantive recommendations to the Task Force for consideration..." **July 20, 1985 - Classified Confidential, Declassified 11/27/92**

The Vice President, being an old Navy salt, appointed the recently retired Chief of Naval Operations (CNO), a 4-star Admiral as Executive Director...for purposes of this Chronicle he will hereafter be referred to as "The Admiral" and the Vice President's Task Force on Combatting Terrorism will be referred to as "The VP Task Force" or just plain "Task Force." Being a military man, the Admiral decided that the primary worker bees would be 05/06's from the Army, Navy, Air Force, Marines, Joint Staff, and the Coast Guard (emphasizing Joint Service cooperation and not a Navy collusion) and he so tasked the Pentagon to make it happen. In turn, the JCS tasked the services to each provide a body, "It should be an excellent opportunity for some of our best talent to gain valuable experience and exposure as well as allow the Services and the Joint Staff to stay closely connected to this important effort." Additionally, the State Department provided a former Ambassador to act as Deputy Director, and from the intelligence community a CIA operations officer...all full time until further notice. The FBI and FAA were asked to give up bodies only part time. Administration staffers from the Navy and CIA rounded out the motley crew.

The Admiral called the first kickoff meeting to be held at a town house at 730 Jackson Place, across Pennsylvania Avenue from the White House next to Lafayette Square...this would turn out to be the operating headquarters of the Task Force for the duration of the effort. Oh, and by the way, civilian attire, no uniforms. After pondering this new adventure,

Sluggo thought, "This is really a big deal that calls for my best behavior; I guess I'll need to buy some suits and stuff and clean up my act." Although the Task Force was a lot of intense work and long hours there were also some not so serious events and a few hijinks, some of which will be revealed in this Chronicle.

And so, the kickoff meeting was conducted, complete with the usual dog sniffing that occurs when a diverse group meets for the first time. The Admiral, whose father was also a CNO and the founder of ROTC, was quite an old school gentleman and very sharp. He began the meeting with objectives, schedule, staff instructions, security (classification up to Top Secret/SCI would be the norm) and other information…this guy was really organized. Some brief words on the Working Group, i.e. crew dogs, a Navy SEAL Captain from JCS, a big guy, call sign "Cuda", a Navy Captain Intel spook, a fine chap for a Navy guy (he and Sluggo became good friends and still are to this day), an Army Colonel artillery type…boom, a Marine Lt Col former Rhodes Scholar, a secret squirrel from CIA (a great guy), and yours truly Lt Col Sluggo, ex BUFF driver. A former ambassador from State would be the Admiral's Deputy, a Lt Commander Coastie helicopter pilot would be the Admiral's executive officer/chief of staff and four admin people including a super woman from CIA would run the paper flow, classified and other…what a job that would prove to be…and she did it exceptionally well!

Some words about the town house, one of 13 similar buildings that lined Jackson Place. Built in the late 1800's, used by the White House for commissions and special projects, including the VP Task Force, two connected to the Blair House, another was occupied by the White House Historical Society, you get the drift. Three stories and a

basement, with ornate woodwork and fixtures, marble fireplaces in the main rooms, and other historic stuff. The first floor of 730 harbored a reception area, the Admiral's office and a large briefing room. The second floor held the Ambassador's office, an admin area and another briefing room. The third floor held the crew dogs; Sluggo, Army, and Cuda in one large suite overlooking the park, and Navy, Jarhead, and Secret Agent in the back suite. The basement would be the catch all area meeting/lunch room, frig and coffee, bunches of safes, and other equipment. A great functional setup...except for one minor thing...there was no bathroom/can/head/loo...as, back in the day when it was built, that facility was in the back yard. And now the fix, the townhouse next door had been upgraded with the necessary facilities, there was a connecting door on the

second floor with access to their heads both men and women. Since the Task Force activities were highly classified and the guys next door were doing a study on the vanishing prairie dog or some other such drivel, there was a one-way door with cypher lock. The gang could get into theirs, but they couldn't get into the task force spaces, and they weren't very happy; lots of stink eye (pun) when passing them in the hallway. The boys weren't very friendly either, if asked what we were doing, we would just say, "Sorry we can't talk about that, but you have a nice bathroom"...a mutual adoration society.

During a frenzy of activity getting the place set up, phones, copiers, etc. it was noted there were no word processors or computers except a couple in admin...the Admiral groused, "This is unsatisfactory." After checking, the White House IT nerds said it might take several months to hook them into their system; the Admiral asked the troops, "Any ideas?" Sluggo piped up and said, "I just had a Wang system installed in my old office in the Pentagon, I can call the Wang lady and see if we could lease a system." She checked it out and said "yes" and it happened in two days with cables snaking up the historic ornate staircases from the basement to the top floor, and it worked great, a box at everyone's desk...and printers.

On their second staff meeting, the Admiral laid out the game plan, quite intense; conduct interviews with very senior officials both government and private sector with any connection to combatting terrorism (CT). Review and visit all government agencies with CT connections, visit and discuss terrorism with foreign governments (Europe, Middle East, Asia), poll the American public to determine the grass roots attitude concerning terrorism. Compile four reports; Top Secret, Secret, Official Business, and Unclassified for public release. And by the way, do it in six months...any questions? The Admiral also assigned areas of responsibilities to the boys, Sluggo was to be the master of media relations and public affairs. "Why me" he reflected, "it couldn't be my outgoing personality… I see plenty of trouble ahead with this gig." The other boys received other similar noncombat tasks, such as interview coordinator, visit coordinator, librarian, government, military, academia, and civilian meeting coordinators, and other such efforts. "Go forth guys, take no prisoners, and win the Task Force war on terrorism," quote the Admiral.

At the next staff meeting, the Admiral said, "put on your finest duds and brush your teeth, the Vice President wants to meet you boys and discuss his ideas with you in his office in the

Old Executive Office Building (OEOB) in the White Hours complex." (now renamed the Eisenhower Executive Office Building). Just a few words about the OEOB. The building was built between 1871 and 1888 in the French Second Empire style, and was called the State, War, and Navy Building because it housed the Departments of State, War, and the Navy, "That's original thinking"

mused Sluggo. It was for years the world's largest office building, with 566 rooms and about ten acres of floor space. Sluggo again mused, "It is so ugly that it's not. The interior however is breathtaking especially the Indian Treaty

Room." The OEOB was referred to by Mark Twain as "the ugliest building in America" and President Harry S. Truman called it "the greatest

monstrosity in America." Vice Presidents since Lyndon Johnson and the Executive Offices of the President have maintained offices there and still do. At the time, little did Sluggo know that he would be attending meetings in that distinguished building for many years to come.

And so, the fateful day came, the Admiral said, "I want you guys to line up and one at a time meet the VP, shake his hand, give a 30 second

bio, and tell him what your job is on the Task Force; then we'll all sit down and for about the next hour, I'll outline the process going forward and ask his guidance and direction," and so they did. Navy Intel was first, he shook the Vice President's hand and said "Mister Pres Viceadent it's a pleasure to meet you" the Captain turned bright red, the VP laughed and grasped his arm, the rest of us had

a more subdued chuckle...no harm, no foul. When it was SEAL Cuda's turn, he said "Sir, I'm the Task Force librarian, I've sent terrorism articles

and suggested reading around to these guys with a buck slip for them to initial and they either don't sign it or send disgusting comments back to me." The VP laughed again a little louder

this time; the ice was broken and remained so for the duration of the Task Force...what a great and personable guy, the meeting was a big success, one of many before they were done.

Time to get to work. The first order of business was to define "Terrorism." After several days of heated debate, the boys determined that effort was like determining how many angels can dance on the head of a pin. You'll know it's terrorism when you see it, or it happens, so let's press on to more important issues. Next, an end to end review of the existing national program to counter terrorism…all Federal Departments, Agencies and Congress. Consultations with individuals acknowledged as experts in the field of terrorism, government, civilian, foreign, industry, and academic. Survey public literature, opinion, and the media. Travel to and consult with foreign allies. Formulate and coordinate recommendations for approval of the Senior Review Group. Construct the final report to the President for the signature of the VP and do it all in six months. "No hill for a climber except for the quicksand," thought Sluggo, "let the consultations with the experts begin."

Most of the consultations took place in the meeting rooms at Jackson Place. When the dust settled the group had interviewed over 100 experts, a few names come to mind, Brzezinski, Eagleburger, Helms, Kissinger, Perot, Smith, Haig, Vessey; and Congressmen, CEOs, Admirals, Generals, Ambassadors, and interestingly, a Marine LtCol from the National Security Council (NSC) staff who Sluggo remembered from the Pentagon…quite a diverse and motley crew. The boys also received briefings from 28 government agencies and visited 14 operations centers in DC and other government entities outside Washington, Ft Bragg and other military bases. Members of the group visited 12 countries in Asia, Europe, and the Middle East and were briefed by the U.S. ambassadors and the foreign government hosts. Sluggo and Army traveled to Germany, Italy, and Spain and met with the U.S. Embassy and the host country counterterrorism officials and their CT response forces including the German GSG 9, Italian GIS, and Spanish GEO. Tough duty but someone had to do it.

You might recall that Sluggo's major tasks were public affairs and media relations. He met with the Vice President's press secretary and staff to develop a game plan. They decided that they would refer Task Force questions from the media direct to Sluggo and together they developed generic Q and A's for response. Soon he started getting phone calls from the fourth estate, not too much of a distraction with one exception. A reporter from a large national daily newspaper was a real pest, she called three or four times a day or more.

"Anything new, how's it going, any nuggets that you would like to share, will you make your suspense, when

can we meet," on and on you get the point. Sluggo devised a plan, the next time she called he arranged to meet her. "You can recognize me, I'll be wearing a dark suit and a green striped tie, sitting on a park bench in Layfette Square off Jackson Place at noon tomorrow eating a bag of carrots (healthy snacks) and I'd like the meeting to be on background." Sluggo assembled some Task Force fact sheets on terrorism complete with some

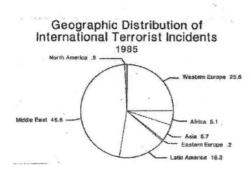

pie charts and bar graphs and put them in a non-descript envelope with her name on it. They met and Sluggo gave her the goods. A day or so later, the charts and graphs and a short article appeared on the front page of her publication. Obviously, at some point, she learned that the information she received was the standard stuff

that she could have gotten if she'd come to the front door of the townhouse and alas, Sluggo never heard from her again.

It wasn't all work and no play as the boys were known to have a few brews after hours in the townhouse basement. The Vice President and the Admiral invited the crew to their private club for a relaxing evening of chili, cornbread and a few libations. The club was in a nondescript three story dark, red brick townhouse, marked with only a street number, a couple of blocks around the corner from the White House. A sign above the door inside stated this club provides "defense against queries by curious men and women," and "he who enters here leaves rank and precedence behind." For years there was no telephone, communication was only by messenger. The club was founded in 1884 and was limited to 50 members including Presidents, Supreme Court Justices, Senators, Generals and Admirals, and other distinguished gentlemen...someone must die to initiate a new member.

The club is decorated with over 100 years of precious junk or as the story goes, it looks as though "it's furnished with everything the Smithsonian ever rejected" and "it's all those things our wives wouldn't let us keep at home." Sluggo thought, "This stuff is incredible," an elephant foot umbrella stand, a framed chastity belt with a curtain, cannonballs and firearms, whole stuffed animals and heads, model ships, planes and trains, the skull of a tiger and thousands more great artifacts every guy would love. Sluggo thought, "If these walls could talk, what a history lesson." A good time was had by all, a great night soaring with eagles.

The VP's press secretary called the Admiral and Sluggo in and advised them that the boss wanted to meet with the major media heavies, editors, bureau chiefs, etc. a small group, only the big boys, and he wants to do it at his quarters at the U.S. Naval Observatory on a Saturday...so go make it

happen Sluggo. (Since VP Mondale, the restored 7,000 sq. ft. elegant mansion at 1 Observatory Circle has been the official resident of the Vice President). On their way back to the townhouse, the Admiral smiled and jokingly asked Sluggo if he knew what he would be doing for the next few weeks.

Letters, memos, and a million phone calls later, here was the line-up; from the Washington Post, Ben Bradlee leading the pack, and Bureau Chiefs and Editors from CNN, U.S. News, UPI, ABC, CBS, NBC, NY Times, Time, Newsweek, and AP. The day came to pass, the VP wanted the discussion to be on the record, but the media heavies insisted it be on background, "What a turnabout," the VP laughed. For nearly two hours, they discussed the role of the media in reporting terrorism…the meeting was an unqualified success. All the Task Force crew dogs attended, and they had a nice chat with the Vice President in parting.

As the months passed the boys were totally committed to putting pen to paper and constructing the final report. It was Christmas time and formal invitations came from the Vice President requesting the Task Force attend his family Christmas party in the residence at the Observatory from 4:00 to 6:00 on a Saturday afternoon. The guys thought that was a rather odd time, it must be the party for the slugs and the big boys party starts later. It turned out the guys were wrong as the cabinet heavies showed up; it seemed that the big White House party was also that night. The place was decorated to the nines and the Army coral singers dressed in Revolutionary period costumes were strolling around singing carols. At one point, the Vice President's wife stood on the stairs and voiced, "What's the matter with you people, join in and sing" and they did… what a lady.

In the main room there was a very large table with all the required foodstuffs, turkeys, ham, roast beast and other goodies. It was beautifully decorated with ornaments and candles and pine boughs hanging from the ceiling. Sluggo was standing near the table sipping a scotch and water (a rather weak one) and chatting with one of the wives when he noticed a candle on the table had tipped and was in the process of lighting the pine boughs on fire. Sluggo calmly stepped around the lady and threw his drink on the small blaze putting the fire out. People were staring at him like what is this idiot doing until they saw what had happened. The Vice President's wife congratulated him with "Thanks, that could have been very serious."

One last story. The Vice President thought an independent, non-government survey of U.S. public opinion on terrorism could be an important part of the Task Force findings. A prominent New York public relations firm was hired to conduct focus group sessions in the East and Midwest with the topic being the "Terrorism: Viewpoint of the American People" and Sluggo would be their Task Force point of contact. After they completed the survey, the decision was made to brief the President and available cabinet members with their findings. Sluggo was responsible to make sure that the physical requirements of the briefing were taken care of. The President's schedule was blocked, and the event was to be held in the White House Situation Room spaces. The briefing room was small, able to hold about 30 people with technical state of the art zero, there was a shelf in the back for a projector and pull-down screen in the front by the entry door and that was it.

Sluggo called New York as they would give the brief and he was informed that the presentation would be on 35mm slides and require a carousal projector with remote and they would fly down on the morning shuttle with the slides. Sluggo thought, "They're only briefing the President, that's no big deal to them I guess, but my ass is on the line if there are any screwups." Sluggo asked them to courier the slides down the day before and they did. Now for his next trick, after he received the slides, finding a projector and carousal tray. The Sit Room guys said, "We don't have one of those projectors, we use overhead viewgraphs." Sluggo spent the next few hours running around the White House complex looking for a projector, he finally found one in the OEOB, but minus a slide tray, he thought he might have to buy one but found one later in another office. Back to the situation room to get everything set up, pull down the screen and project…and it all worked. The President's chair was at the head of the table directly in front of the screen, so his chair was moved around the side.

The fateful day came, the Big Apple people got there on time and the heavy breathers began to assemble in the Sit Room. At the required time, the President arrived. He walked into the room and noticed that his chair was missing, and the screen was down, he remarked to the VP, "Is this a coup George or we going to watch one of my great old films?" The Attorney General piped up and said "yes, your monkey movie – Bedtime for Bonzo." After a bit of banter between POTUS and his boys, a good laugh was had by all and the brief went well, the meeting was a roaring success, Sluggo thought, "I really dodged a bullet on this escapade."

After six months of frantic work, the boys finalized the report for the coordination of the heavies. They found over 150 government entities were involved in some manner to combat terrorism, employing thousands of people and spending billions annually…lots of sacred rice bowls. Believe it or not, the coordination process went well even with the substance of the report that heavily tasked many of the Federal Departments and Agencies with actions and change. The report contained 44 major recommendations to improve U.S. policy. After lots of debate and changing happy to glad, on January 6, 1986, the Senior Review Group passed the report to the Cabinet who in turn passed it to the Vice President for the President. On January 20, 1986, the President signed out a Top Secret, National Security Decision Directive 207 (NSDD 207), The National Program for Combatting Terrorism.

NSDD 207 ~ THE NATIONAL PROGRAM FOR COMBATTING TERRORISM

"The Vice President's Task Force on Combatting Terrorism has completed an in-depth review of our current policies, capabilities, and resources for dealing with the terrorist threat. I have reviewed the Task Force Report...I have determined that we must enhance our ability to confront this threat...they made numerous recommendations to further our capabilities. Accordingly, I have made the following decisions...the recommendations of the Vice President's Task Force on Combatting Terrorism are to be fully and consistently implemented..."
January 20, 1986, Classified Top Secret, Declassified 8/25/08

After the NSDD was published, the Admiral asked if the guys could stick around for several months to construct the unclassified public report of the Task Force (published in February 1986) and other actions to close down the Task Force. Sluggo asked the Air Staff (he was still assigned to them) for permission and they didn't have any problem with that, "Just let us now when you think you will be done."   During a conversation with the Admiral, the Vice President passed along a request "Your guys have done a great job, they are true experts on terrorism and the current government CT policy process, I would like to keep them   around   in   the

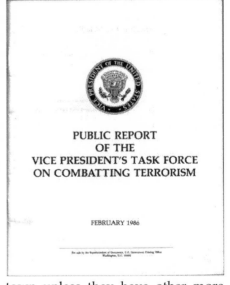

**PUBLIC REPORT
OF THE
VICE PRESIDENT'S TASK FORCE
ON COMBATTING TERRORISM**

FEBRUARY 1986

counterterrorism business here in town unless they have other more important career moves." The Admiral passed the word down and the guys made their choices, Sluggo wanted to go to the NSC as did two of the other chaps. After the meeting, the Admiral took Sluggo aside and said, "I've been impressed with your performance these past months and in my opinion, you would be a better fit at the State Department rather than with the current NSC crowd. I think the Office of the Ambassador at

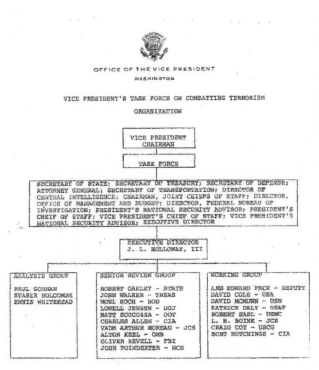

Large for Counterterrorism at State would welcome you with open arms, you will give them a positive perspective on the military and help them implement their NSDD 207 taskings." Sluggo thought, "That has to beat Omaha, and although I've never had much tact, I guess I could learn something from the striped pants diplomats...if the Air Force agrees, I'll do it," and they did and so did he. As he was to learn later, not going to the NSC Staff really saved his bacon, big time.

Chapter Twenty: State Department — "How Sluggo Learned Tact, Diplomacy and How to Eat Quiche"

As opposed to previous Chronicles, this issue isn't as action packed with the usual hijinks as Sluggo epistles of the past have been ... sadly the mid-80's were not mirthful times in our Nations' Capitol. Here's some stories, some may make you smile, some may piss you off, some may not. Names have been changed/omitted to protect the innocent and the guilty...you figure it out.

Sluggo, as discussed, spent nearly a year at the White House as a member of the Working Group of the Vice President's Task Force on Combatting Terrorism. These efforts resulted in the classified NSDD 207, signed by the President, containing 44 recommendations to enhance the unified fight against terrorism. As one of the key recommendations was to improve interagency cooperation, the working group members were reassigned to key positions within the DC area. Although Sluggo's first choice was the NSC, going to State instead saved him much grief and other things.

But not so fast slick, you're not going to just stroll in there; the Ambassador at Large for Counterterrorism would like to interview you. Sluggo had met the Ambassador several times during the Task Force work, in fact, he was the State member of the Task Force Senior Review Group. The interview went well, the Ambassador was especially interested in Sluggo's experience in exercises and emergency management. "As you know, National Security Decision Directive 30 designates the State Department as lead agency for counterterrorism overseas, it also tasks me to lead the Interdepartmental Group on Terrorism (IG/T) and to conduct a counterterrorism exercise program, with your operational background and Pentagon experience you would be a great addition to this Office, welcome aboard."

NSDD 30 ~ <u>Managing Terrorist Incidents</u>

- *<u>Lead Agency</u>: The State Department, for international terrorist incidents that take place outside of U.S. territory.*
- *<u>The Interdepartmental Group on Terrorism (IG/T)</u>: chaired by the Department of State, will be responsible for the development of overall U.S. policy on terrorism, …and interagency training programs.*
- *<u>Planning and Exercises</u>: To ensure effective management of terrorism incidents, prior planning and exercise activity are essential. IG/T will be the primary mechanism within the U.S. Government for planning and policy recommendations…the Chairman of the IG/T will appoint an Exercise Committee which will coordinate the development of a multi-year exercise program.* **Signed by the President, April 10, 1982 ~ Classified Secret, Declassified May 3, 1999**

Greetings from "Foggy Bottom"… Foggy Bottom is thought to have received its name due to its Potomac riverside location, which made it susceptible to concentrations of fog, industrial smoke, and low hanging haze…it also smelled very bad, but that's another story. In the early 1930s, a decision was made to develop the land as the War Department (WD) Headquarters and so construction began. But wait, WW II erupted and WD said," the new buildings are too small, we're going to move across the river to Virginia and construct a monster five-sided building and call it the Pentagon – State Department, it's all yours." "Thanks, we'll take it" said the diplomats. Building the complex continued for years, when completed it was named in honor of President Harry S. Truman, 8,000 worker bees now inhabit the facility. State was the primary occupant of Foggy Bottom back in the day; thus, the

Department is often referred to as "Foggy Bottom," that's a metonym…look it up, Sluggo had to. In 1910, Congress passed an Act restricting the heights of buildings in DC. That's why most of the DC

Federal buildings are seven stories high. Since the seat of power in the world usually occupies the high ground, the seventh floor in most DC

Federal agencies is where the heavy breathers live..."I just got called up to the 'seventh floor'...am I in trouble?" another metonym. The Secretary of State also lives on the 7th floor but wait, there was an 8th floor in one part of the building that was used for serious diplomatic meetings, receptions, and all that jazz. It was quite impressive featuring priceless early American furniture and artwork and other regal stuff. "Very nice" thought Sluggo, "But I bet they won't let me eat my lunch up there."

The Ambassador took Sluggo around to meet the troops, the official designation of the office was S/CT, the S indicating a direct report to the

Secretary of State, the CT, you can figure that out. The office was about 25 strong, a mix of Foreign Service Officers (FSOs), Civil Service folks,

and another military guy, an Air Force Lt Col C-130 driver who was about to depart, but not before he gave Sluggo some sage FSO wisdom. "FSOs are an interesting lot as a result of several Acts of Congress over the years they have their own empire, different pay, promotion, retirement, etc., than the rest of the government slugs, you get the idea...all in all a secure rice bowl...also, some can be very sold on themselves." During their weeding out process, FSOs take a very rigorous test for selection, only 50-pound brains need apply thank you.

Besides the Ambassador at Large, the big boss, (an Ambassador at Large is appointed by the President) there was also a just plain Ambassador deputy. The office was roughly divided into Operations, Policy, and Public Affairs. Sluggo joined the Ops staff, first task; rejuvenate the national counterterrorism exercise program which had been on the back burner for a while and strengthen the Emergency

Support Team (EST) that deployed during counterterrorism ops, more about the EST later.

After he started at State, the Air Force called Sluggo to inform him that his Officer Efficiency Report (OER) from the VP Task Force had been signed by the Vice President but he had failed to enter his social security number (SSN) on the form, could he do anything about it. "I'll just call him up and tell him to redo it, he doesn't have anything else to do, he's only the VP," he thought. Sluggo replied "I'm not working there anymore, and I don't think I can do anything about it." He never heard from the AF again and the signed OER minus the VP's SSN appeared in his records.

It was a very tumultuous and interesting time with lots of moving parts, so before we continue with the hijinks; a shallow dive into the past. "Is oil the root of all evil? maybe it's one of them" thought Sluggo. The following is not meant to be a history lesson, but in Sluggo's opinion, some of the basic reasons why we got thrown in this briar patch; not our finest hour.

- Rumor has it that U.S. and British intelligence orchestrated a coup in Iran, the pro-western Shah emerged as ruler, leading to a rapid industrial and military modernization as well as economic and social reforms. The secret squirrel mantra was at work, *Admit Nothing, Deny Everything, Make Counter Accusations.*

- Iran our new best friend; why Iran? Strategic location, Persian Gulf, long common boarders with the dreaded Soviets and of course oil.

- Iranians bought the most state-of-the-art weapons systems available from the U.S. and U.K. including; F-4 fighter/bombers, Chieftain

tanks, TOW antitank missiles, HAWK ground-to-air missile systems, and F-14 Tomcat interceptors with Phoenix air-to-air missiles...*I feel the need...the need for speed.*

• 1979, goodbye Shah, we hated to see you go. Iranian Revolution, government overthrown by secular and religious fanatics. *Islamic Republic of Iran* proclaimed. Our old friend…our new worst enemy now a state sponsor of terrorism. Serious U.S. economic sanctions, embargo on arms, and no spare parts for your toys, take that Iran.

• 1979, We don't like you or your President U.S., so take this….*Imam Line* extremist student supporters seize U.S. Embassy Tehran, Iran. 52 Americans taken hostage.

• 1980, *Operation Eagle Claw*, U.S. Tehran hostage rescue mission fails…ends in disaster.

• 1980, Iran/Iraq War. Saddam Hussein determines Iranian Revolution has weakened their military…shortages of spare parts for Iran's U.S and British-made arms has crippled their once-mighty military. With his state-of-the-art Soviet arms, he invades Iran. Of these two bombasters, who do we despise the most?

• 1981, Tehran hostage crisis spells the end of the Carter Administration, President Reagan elected, hostages released after 444 days captive.

• 1982, Lebanon Civil War, Christian West vs. Islamic East. *Hezbollah* was born; a radical extremist terrorist group who pioneered suicide bombings; was manned, armed, and funded by Iran. Goal; end American, French, and Western presence in Lebanon.

• 1982, Israel invades Lebanon, supports the Christians, and "Don't screw with us PLO."

• 1982, Lebanon hostage crisis, directed by Iran, *Hezbollah* begins taking foreigners hostage in Beirut by the dozens. Widespread outrage fueled by the media in the U.S.… "We need to do something."

• 1983, Beirut Lebanon, Embassy suicide bombings; French 58 killed; U.S., 75 killed including 17 Americans. *Hezbollah* takes credit.

• 1983, Beirut Lebanon, suicide bombing French Barracks, 58 killed; and U.S. Marine Corps Battalion Landing Team compound, 217 U.S. Service personnel killed. *Hezbollah* again.

• 1984, Mediterranean Sea, Italian cruise ship *Achille Lauro* hijacked, crippled Jewish American civilian murdered, thrown overboard in his wheelchair to his death. *Hezbollah*.

• 1985, Trans World Airlines Flight 847 hijacked by *Hezbollah*, U.S. Navy diver executed in Beirut, passengers held captive in Lebanon for two weeks.

- 1985 Vice President's Task Force on Combatting Terrorism issues report.
- 1986, Sluggo moves to the Department of State. "You'll need a bunch of programs to figure out who all the players are in this crazy game," thought Sluggo, "and alas, I'm right in the middle of it."

Sluggo hit the ground running, his new office was at a fever pitch; terrorism against the U.S. was running rampant in Europe and the Middle East, and Americans were being held hostage in Lebanon. Thus, accelerated ongoing critical planning and exercising responses to terrorism, both diplomatic and military. State was well organized to respond to these contingencies, their Operations Center on the 7th floor was divided into three separate 24/7 "Task Force" areas able to handle three different emergencies at the same time. Sluggo was soon integrated into the system, "I have a feeling that I'll be spending some time up here" he thought...more than you think ace. During one contingency around 2:00 am, Sluggo looked around and thought "Most of the Task Force members here are military and I'm the senior guy so I'm now running the State Department, so I think I could make a diplomatic declaration...but I probably won't."

Sluggo had a nice office on the second floor with a window...impressive. The office was one floor above the exit from the underground parking garage reserved for the heavies and foreign diplomats. The exit was protected by a pop-up barrier, one afternoon there was a tremendous noise and you guessed it, a limo was impaled by the barrier, box seats in Sluggo's office and some pissed off foreign diplomats.

One perk for being military and working at State was parking, located across the street was the U.S. Navy Bureau of Medicine and Surgery a complex called *Navy Hill* and yes, designated parking at no cost to military toads. This perk required taking a sacred oath not to discuss the same around State employees, most who had no parking or paid big bucks for commercial parking, enough said. *Navy Hill* had an interesting history, it was the original headquarters of the Office of Strategic Services (OSS) of WW II, Wild Bill Donovan fame. And later, the first home of the Central Intelligence Agency…it's rumored that sneaky stuff still goes on over there, I wonder?

Sluggo was also integrated into the EST. The EST was an interagency group responsible for deploying to terrorist incidents worldwide, wheels up in four hours. Led by State; members included CIA, FBI, Defense and other agencies joining depending on the crisis; if weapons of mass destruction, (bugs, gas, or nukes). For example, if the threat was radiological, the Department of Energy (DOE) team would deploy (Sluggo began a relationship with DOE that would continue for many years). The EST provided specialized crisis response expertise to augment existing U.S. Mission and host government capabilities and to assist and advise the U.S. Chief of Mission in assessing the contingency and coordinating U.S. government crisis response. The EST also brought secure Satcom radios, a direct line to DC and other crisis related stuff. Sluggo, being Air Force, would function as a hook into the Pentagon to get transportation, usually a USAF C-141 with satellite communication. Meeting the four-hour wheels up goal was always a problem.

The long pole in the deployment tent was airlift as no aircraft were specifically dedicated to the mission and one had to be plucked from the Military Airlift Command (MAC) flow. To be more effective the team needed a dedicated aircraft which eventually happened as there were lots of old tired Boeing 707's and T-43's (USAF version of the 737) flying around out there. The first mobilization exercise of the EST with the dedicated 707 went down one summer evening. The plan was to rendezvous at a major hotel parking lot adjacent to a major Washington airport where the plane was parked, load up and travel to the jet and see how long the whole thing would take. The recall went well and about 25 of the boys all decked out in their various black and scary ninja gear and kit started to assemble in the parking lot with lots of other equipment including a box truck full of high-speed stuff. Since no one bothered letting the hotel know, they feared an invasion or worse, someone called the local cops who showed up with lights flashing and siren blaring. After a lot of "show me your badge and I'll show you mine" the problem was solved...no harm, no foul ... and "you guys really don't want to know what's in that truck." Rather reminiscent of the old Keystone Cops flicks. More on EST exercises later.

There were lots of "behind the green door" antics going on in DC. The Iran/Iraq war wasn't going so well for the Iranians, because of the arms embargo they were using up munitions and lots of their high-tech U.S. war stuff was breaking with no spare parts. Enter the Lebanon American hostage crisis...constant rescue attempt planning, but where are they? No one knew for sure. U.S. response to *Hezbollah* terrorism was on

the front burner but what to do; they have our people locked up. And a spate of international terrorism directed against the U.S., especially the American military worldwide...do something...now.

Here's the tale in a nutshell. The NSC big boss was advised that Iran

needed assistance in their battle with Iraq and if the West doesn't help, the Soviets might jump in. He proposed to help but many of the Cabinet heavies didn't think it was a good idea. His staff, the inner circle composed of a boat load of *Canoe U* (USNA) graduates thought it was a great idea and took it for action. "Since Iran needs U.S. weapons, and Iran controls the *Hezbollah* in Lebanon, and the *Hezbollah* is holding Americans hostage, let us trade arms for hostages. But how can we sell munitions to Iran with an arms embargo in place and the fact that the U.S. has declared Iran a state sponsor of terrorism. Since we're selling the same stuff to Israel that Iran wants, let's see if Israel will sell the stuff to Iran and we'll backfill the Israeli equipment and they can pass the money from Iran back to us." After lots of toing and froing Israel said "Yes" and Iran said, "Yes and we'll tell our proxy *Hezbollah* to release U.S. hostages," and so it began with those unmarked 707's flying around the Middle East doing their thing. The cutouts required to make all this happen included a collection of seedy and disreputable characters of all nationalities. The first shipment of 96 U.S. made TOW missiles was delivered, three weeks later 408 more TOW's were delivered. Following the second delivery, an American missionary held hostage was released from Beirut.

By now, the NSC big boss had enough and resigned, his pipe smoking side kick deputy and his merry men took over running the NSC. The arms shipments went on including U.S. made HAWK missiles. There were lots of fits and starts with hostage releases, but they were slowly starting to dribble out. The NSC gang thought what are we going to do with all this money in Swiss accounts and other places. One particular NSC staffer had a fixation with the situation in Central America. The U.S. intelligence agencies had been supporting the Contra "freedom fighters" in efforts to overthrow the Nicaraguan government. Congress said not so fast and passed the Boland Amendments: *"During the fiscal year 1985 no funds available to the*

The New York Times introduction to the *Tower Commission Report* pictures "a National Security Council led by reckless cowboys off on a wild ride, taking direct operational control of matters that are customarily province of more sober agencies such as the CIA, State, and Defense. In this instance, the report says, a kind of parallel government came into being, operating in secret, paying scant heed to laws, deceiving Congress and avoiding oversight of any kind. The NSC senior leadership the report adds, "functioning largely outside the orbit of the U.S. Government," acting through a shadowy network of Americans, Israelis, and Iranians, some of whom were considered most unreliable by senior U.S. officials."

New York Times
SPECIAL

THE TOWER COMMISSION REPORT

THE FULL TEXT OF THE
PRESIDENT'S SPECIAL
REVIEW BOARD

JOHN TOWER, Chairman
EDMUND MUSKIE and
BRENT SCOWCROFT, members

Introduction by
R. W. APPLE, JR.
Chief Washington Correspondent of
The New York Times

Central Intelligence Agency, the Department of Defense or any other agency or entity of the United States involved in intelligence activities may be obligated or expended for the purpose of or which may have the effect of supporting directly or indirectly military or paramilitary operations in Nicaragua by any nation, organization, group, movement, or individual."

"That certainly doesn't apply to the NSC" thought the boys, "We're not an intelligence agency, why don't we use some of that Iranian money to buy guns for the Contras." Enter another cast of sleezy and disreputable arms dealers and more unmarked airplanes. But alas, for a variety of reasons, the *Iran Contra* balloon burst, and the Tower Commission was born to investigate the fiasco, what a read. The whole affair was like the unbelievable plot of a pulp novel…and you can't make this stuff up. In the immortal words of Laurel and Hardy, "Well, here's another nice mess you've gotten me into."

Back to Sluggo and State, the guys in S/CT had pretty much figured out the arms for hostage operation, but they didn't see the Contra show coming. About the U.S. hostages in Lebanon, since they were starting to be released, a special interagency protocol was developed for their recovery. They were usually moved by Navy helicopter (the U.S. had a substantial Naval presence in the Med) to Larnaca Airport, Cyprus (an old RAF base) where they were met by U.S. officials and usually a waiting USAF C-9 MedEvac aircraft. Then they were airlifted to the USAF Regional Medical Center in Wiesbaden Germany for medical evaluation and debriefings conducted by the usual suspects from Washington; who were your captors, where were you held hostage, anything else important? Then on to Andrews

AFB via USAF Military Airlift Command C-141 for appropriate receptions...of course the NSC was deeply involved in all of that for whatever reason. Sluggo was tasked to make sure that all the AF airlift was moving smoothly and had since he had an Andrews AFB flight line ramp pass, he was also involved in the reception process back in DC.

During one such release, when he informed his old Task Force buddies at the NSC that he had a C-9 Medevac on alert to pick up the hostage, he was told that they had chartered a Swiss Lear Jet, it was waiting in Larnaca, and they would move the hostage to Germany. Sluggo said, "that's a breach in the protocol, your infamous NSC crony wouldn't possible be on that airplane would he?"...pregnant silence was the

answer. Sluggo met that hostage on the Andrews flight line later in the week.

For one hostage release, he was tasked to lead the debriefing team to Wiesbaden, according to the protocol the C-141 aircraft would fly them to Germany and wait until the debriefing was over then fly

everyone back to Andrews. After landing the 141 aircrew informed Sluggo that MAC wanted to put the dedicated aircraft back into the normal Europe air flow schedule. Sluggo asked, "What would you guys rather do, go back to hauling trash for MAC or spend a few days in the land of schnitzel and beer"...enough said, "I'll take care of Mother MAC"...and he did, and the C-141 crew dogs had a merry time.

Sluggo was soon appointed chairman of the Interagency Counterterrorism Exercise Committee, there are many wonderful exercise

stories but here's a few specific morsels. In light of the Beirut situation, the exercise flavor of the year was of course hostage rescue. During an exercise at Fort Ord on the California coast (check out a map, the California coast terrain looks similar to Lebanon) Sluggo role played the U.S. Ambassador in Beirut. One of the objects of the bad guys (played by Army Special Forces) was to take him hostage. Sluggo managed to evade them by having two rooms in different motels and one room in the BOQ and messing up the beds and bathroom in all the places to confuse the boys. They were also easy to make with all the same model rental cars only of different colors...the red one just left, here comes the blue one. For sure they would have kicked his ass if captured, bag on head, flex ties on wrists, and more indignities, sorry Army, not today.

The island of Antigua was selected (with their government approval) for the site of a maritime terrorism exercise. SEALs would be assault force with two targets, a very large rented yacht in the harbor and a huge villa on the shore, terrorists were holding hostages in both locations. Various U.S. snake eaters and spooks deployed and began gathering intelligence. Sluggo and the EST deployed and began to set up. The consulate in Antigua, was a nice facility but with little or no security. On a Friday, Sluggo briefed the Consul and told him they needed to setup on Saturday and Sunday, he replied, "We don't work on the weekend, here's the keys to the consulate...knock yourselves out." "A trusting soul or something thought Sluggo, I now have the keys to the kingdom." The night of the exercise all hell broke loose; helicopter assaults, flash bangs, fire fights, zooming airplanes, and lots of noise. The government had decided not to let the public know exactly what was happening so lots of speculation. The local

newspaper headlines the next day stated that Vice President Bush was holding a secret meeting with Anwar Sadat of Egypt on the big yacht in the harbor. The exercise was a rousing success, the hostages were rescued, all was well, and the citizens of Antigua were in wonder with lots of theories for weeks to come.

A few changes in the wind for Sluggo, his old Ambassador boss departed, and a new Ambassador at Large arrived, he was a young fast burner, very smart and a super sharp. With him were two just plain Ambassadors acting as Deputies. As it turned out, they both thought Sluggo worked for them, they were both really great guys... so it wasn't a problem as the Sluggo juggling act began.

Will wonders never cease, Sluggo made Colonel...shocker. A pin-on ceremony in the fancy reception area on the eighth floor of State was in order. Sluggo's three-star Air Force boss (soon to be a four star and Chief of Staff of the Air Force) came over to

assist as the new Ambassador looked on. Who is that cute Air Force officer in a skirt...I wonder...could that be Shooter? The Air Force wanted

Sluggo to put his Blue Suit back on, but the new Ambassador wanted Sluggo to stay at State, so he sent a letter to the Secretary of the Air Force (SECAF) asking if Sluggo could extend. SECAF said yes, so more fun at State. The Colonel's Group in AF Personnel wasn't too pleased with that decision...watch out Sluggo.

Perhaps the wildest CT exercise that Sluggo participated in at State was called *Mighty Derringer*. *Mighty Derringer* was indeed mighty, it was the first full blown field exercise of U.S. capabilities to respond to terrorist use of improvised nuclear devices (IND). It was co-sponsored by the Department of Energy (DOE) the keeper of all nuclear things that go boom. The scenario depicted loose nukes in both Indianapolis Indiana and a country south of the U.S. border called Montrev (one guess who that was). FBI was in charge of the Indy event and State was in charge of the Montrev show.

DOE set up Montrev city in an abandoned complex at the Nevada Test Site of nuke boom fame, hundreds of cleared DOE employees speaking only Spanish acted as the population and government officials. All U.S. counterterrorist assets (lots of choppers and other high-speed stuff) and teams were

deployed to the Test Site, including the DOE Nuclear Emergency Search Team (NEST), and Sluggo and the EST. In fact, Sluggo was play acting as the U.S. Ambassador to Montrav for the first half of the exercise until his real Ambassador boss showed up. The leader of Montrev, El Presidente, paraded around for meetings in a stretch black limo with a big red rotating bubble on top. He was always accompanied by two female bodyguards in black flight suits sporting Uzis.

Over the next five days everyone did their thing, the nuke (the DOE boys had constructed a working replica of an IND complete with anti-tampering devices) was finally discovered on the abandoned nuclear rocket test cell, the bad guys were disposed of with extreme prejudice, and the NEST began to render the bomb safe only to find out that it had already gone off. The theory was a bird, or some other varmint had landed on or messed with it setting it off. In spite of that, and the many exercise theatrics, lots of vital lessons learned lasting for years to come were realized from Mighty Derringer. Sluggo also became a fast friend with several of the DOE crew dogs and still is to this day.

One more exercise story. The Summer Olympics were scheduled for Seoul, South Korea, and the threat of a terrorist campaign to disrupt them was a genuine possibility. They asked for U.S. assistance in planning a joint response should an incident happen. On the agenda was a combined counterterrorism field exercise with the elite snake eaters from both countries. The Ambassador tasked Sluggo to attend the planning conference in Seoul. Our boy departed DC for Chicago direct to Seoul, a 16-plus hour adventure. The three-day conference had its ups and downs but finally all agreed on the scenario and exercise events. The Koreans were betting their future on pulling it off with no snags and they really meant it. Sluggo got home on a Saturday afternoon and went into work on Monday. The Ambassador immediately called him into his office and said, "Everything has gone to hell in Korea, get your ass back on an airplane and go fix it." Sluggo asked, "When do you want me to go?" And the Ambassador said "now." Sluggo thought, "I was hoping he wasn't going to say that but knew he would." So back on a plane and back to Seoul. By the time Sluggo got there, most of the problems had almost solved themselves. So, a successful two-hour U.S./Korean meeting at the embassy then a day of shopping in A Tae Won, purchasing some suspicious Nikes, Pumas, Nolex (not a Rolex) watches and other goodies, then back home. "Two trips to Korea and back in a week is a little much, even worse than a 24-hour BUFF mission," bemoaned Sluggo.

International terrorism continued, Libyan goons bombed Europe and us, so we pounded Libya back and Sluggo continued to do his duty in the State Task Force. But the time to put his Blue Suit  back on was long past due. The Ambassador asked the Air Force for one more extension and the Air Force said no. "Back to flying" thought Sluggo..."Not a chance buddy, you're now too senior." He got a call from the almighty Colonel's Group, the flesh peddlers that ruled boy colonels' lives and the gang he had pissed off in the past. They reported that they had a by-name assignment for him (at least someone wanted him) and he was going to the U.S. Pacific Command at Camp H. M. Smith in Hawaii as the Chief of the Command Center Improvement Program. Sluggo said "I don't know anything about that program," the Group responded, "That's not our concern, some senior AF officer (not to be named) asked for you, and you alone, have a nice trip big boy, you're now out of our hair, " they snickered. So Sluggo said his goodbyes, packed his bags and flew off to Aloha Land for whatever fate awaited him. An Air Force colonel, off to a Marine Corps Camp to work for a Navy Admiral, at a job he knows nothing about, it couldn't get any better than that...living the dream and loving the life...anchors aweigh my boys, we sail at break of day.

I wonder what will happen next in the life of our intrepid ex-aviator...it probably won't be flying a BUFF, doing the Hula, or singing with Don Ho...but who knows...

Chapter Twenty-one: CINCPAC – "Our Intrepid Air Force Ex-Aviator Goes to an Island Paradise to Replace an Army Colonel and Work at a Marine Corps Camp for a Navy Admiral at a Job He Knows Nothing About...Any Questions?"

Aloha and Mahalo. Sluggo said his goodbyes to our Nations' Capitol, 1979-1988, the Pentagon, the White House, and State, what a great and fulfilling run...although it did little to further his Air Force career. He was still scratching his head trying to figure out why he was going to be the Chief, Command Center Improvement Program (CCIP)...damn Colonel's Group. He heard through the grape vine that the Group had recently taken his name in vain, "That Sluggo character will do anything to stay in DC including marrying Shooter, the AF Personnel General's Executive Officer, but that's not going to save him this time." Yes, after a Pentagon romance, Sluggo and Shooter got married. Sadly, he had to leave Shooter behind with the promise she would join him as soon as the Air Force could work a joint-spouse assignment for her. So off to Hawaii and the U.S. Marine Corps' Camp H. M. Smith. Sluggo had been to Hawaii and Camp Smith numerous times when working exercises at the Pentagon and State, so no big surprises. First on the agenda, find a place to live, there were no BOQs at Camp Smith so he checked into the Navy BOQ at Makalapa next

to Pearl Harbor just down the hill from Camp Smith, not bad for Navy quarters and a 10-minute ride to work.

Camp H.M. Smith started its life during WW II as Aiea Naval Hospital which was slapped together quickly out of tar paper, spit, and wood to support the casualties inevitable with an invasion of Japan; it was never meant to be a permanent fixture. It did serve as a stopping off place for thousands of wounded sailors and Marines on their way home from the

war in the Pacific. Hospital activity peaked following the battle for Iwo Jima when nearly 6,000 patients received medical care simultaneously. When the war was over, the Marines explained to the Navy, "Since the Army just opened a new modern Joint Military Hospital on the island and we need a home for Fleet Marine Force Pacific (FMFPAC) and this old hospital is going to be empty or something, we're taking this turf over for our headquarters any questions?" And so, it happened. The "Camp" was named for General Holland McTyeire Smith, the first commanding general of FMFPAC. The initials H. M. also stood for his nickname which was "Howling Mad" referring to his temper and so named by his beloved Marines.

Not to totally bore you, but in a nutshell, in military speak, here's the United States Unified Command Plan (UCP). The UCP assigns geographic and functional areas of responsibilities (AORs) throughout the world to designated four-star Generals and Admirals who were called Commanders in Chiefs (CINCs). As the world turns the UCP in turn changes over the years and so does the command structures. In the Pacific in the old days, the four-star Navy Admiral at Makalapa near Pearl Harbor wore two hats, he was both the

Commander of the whole Pacific Joint AOR, and the Commander of the Navy Pacific Fleet. The other Services cried foul, too much power for one big Navy Kahuna, "We've got people in the Pacific also and they get hand-me-downs and; the fleet gets everything," so to keep the peace, the two positions were separated. But wait, two Navy four-stars Flags sharing the same "castle" at Makalapa, that will never work, so in 1957 the Admiral and his 'Joint' Command, Navy, Army, Air Force and Marines, now named USCINCPAC moved to Camp Smith, "So make way Jar Heads we're coming in, and there's plenty of room for both in the old hospital....but you still own the Camp," after the mandatory dog sniffing, the transition went smooth.

But wait, in 2002, Secretary of Defense Donald Rumsfeld (remember him?) directed that the title of "Commander-in-Chief" be reserved <u>solely</u> for the President of the United States, therefore, you all CINCs have to change your names. So, the military heavy breathers changed the names to just plain "Command", so USCINCPAC became Pacific Command or PACOM, in Europe, USCINCEUR became EUCOM, and so forth, you get the idea. (*The name PACOM was just recently changed again to the United States Indo-Pacific Command, INDOPACOM*). Most of this latest commotion occurred after Sluggo's time, so for the rest of this Chronicle and to save ink, INDOPACOM will be referred to CINCPAC. CINCPAC

was and still is the oldest and largest of the United States' Unified Commands, the AOR occupies more than 50 percent of the earth's surface, an area of over 100 million square miles. 36 nations, more than half the world's population,

speaking 3,200 different languages. Whew, I hope you got all that, because there will be a test on the UCP at the end of this missive.

Sluggo's sponsor was the Army Colonel that he was replacing. He was a Signal Corps officer (Army communicator, in charge of GI wire heads and computer nerds). He was a great guy about to transfer to a new Army job on the mainland, he really helped Sluggo get settled. As they talked and compared careers, he said he couldn't figure out what the hell Sluggo was doing in the job as the Chief, CCIP, Sluggo said he didn't know either. The CCIP mission was to turn the Vietnam era command post into a state-of-the-art facility with all the bells and whistles and high-speed, low drag technical stuff. The office consisted of the Chief, some young, 50-pound brain wire head civilians, an older prior enlisted Air Force Captain call sign "Blinky," and a secretary. Surprisingly, and unlike most projects like this, it had significant funding and visibility under the J-6, C3, and thus, a constant flow of contractors wanting to help and sell their wares. The numerical organizational system of the Army had been adapted for the Joint organizations per Goldwater-Nichols. Now, serving in a Joint command was seriously a mandatory square to fill for promotion in the military. Here's the line-up:

- J-1, Personnel and Manpower
- J-2, Intelligence
- J-3, Operations
- J-4, Logistics
- J-5, Strategic Plans and Policy
- J-6, Command, Control, Communications

"The Goldwater–Nichols Department of Defense Reorganization Act 4, 1986 (signed by President Ronald Reagan), made the most sweeping changes to the United States Department of Defense by reworking the command structure of the United States military. It increased the powers of the Chairman of the Joint Chiefs of Staff and streamlined the military chain of command, running from the President through the Secretary of Defense directly to combatant commanders (all four-star generals or admirals), bypassing the services. The Act was an attempt to fix problems caused by inter-service rivalry. Such problems existed in World War II and Korea, had emerged during the Vietnam War, contributed to the catastrophic failure of the Iranian hostage rescue mission in 1980. and was still evident in the invasion of Grenada in 1983."

Sluggo's office was in a strange area of the old building called the basement but it wasn't really a basement because it wasn't underground, and it had windows. Down the hall was a large room used for storage

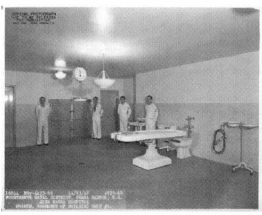

purported to be the morgue of the old hospital and of course it was haunted, strange noises, lights, things moving, standard spook stuff...very scary. It soon became evident that Sluggo needed to learn a new language...Navy Speak. Hallways became passageways, doors became hatches, floors became decks, stairs became ladders, bathrooms became heads, and of course the "Bridge" was the area where all the heavy breathers and movers and shakers lived to drive the boat. And so Sluggo drank from the nerd fire hose to learn the basics of the Navy and CCIP.

Sluggo's new Captain was a pro wrestling fanatic and wait, the unbelievable was happening in Hawaii, the World Wrestling gang including "The Beast" were coming to town. Blinky was so excited he couldn't stop talking about it, and of course Sluggo was invited to be his guest and he was so fired up Sluggo knew he had to go with him. So, the fateful day came and Sluggo and Blinky put on their wrestling togs and made it to the Honolulu International Center Arena which was a complete zoo and packed to the bulkheads (more Navy speak) with screaming fans…who knew that pro wrestling was such a big deal in paradise? After the prelims it was time for the big match featuring "The Beast" and he didn't disappoint. All the standard antics plus more; attacks and blows and punches that would kill a mere mortal within seconds. Watching in person you could really see the lads pulling their punches. Blinky was so excited he was almost in a coma, when Sluggo pointed out the punch pulling he said, "These guys are so good it only looks like they are pulling punches, they're just so fast you just can't see them land." The night ended, and a good time was had by all especially Blinky.

Time flies when you're having fun and Sluggo toiled on with CCIP. Good news, Shooter got her orders, instead of Pacific Air Force as she suspected, she got a Joint assignment and was actually coming soon to Camp Smith to work in J-1, Personnel and Manpower. She was also promoted early to Major, "a fast burner, someone's got a career left," thought Sluggo. But riding to work together, perhaps we'll see. Then a *bolt out of the blue* struck, Sluggo got a call from the office of the Deputy CINCPAC, an Air Force three star general and the highest-ranking AF officer in the Command. "The General would like to see you tomorrow in his office on the bridge, here's the time." Sluggo asked what it was concerning; the answer was, "He'll tell you then." Sluggo racked his pea brain, he didn't know the General and had never crossed paths with him before, was this a standard "meet and greet" or something else, who knows?

Sluggo reported to the Bridge at the appropriate time and was ushered into the General's office (Cabin in Navy speak) and reported in a military manner. The General shook his hand and asked Sluggo to shut the door and take a seat, then it was just the two of them. The General asked Sluggo, "Why do you think you got assigned to this Headquarters in the CCIP job?" Sluggo was at a loss of words. The General continued, "Several months ago I reviewed your records and was impressed with your counterterrorism experience in the Pentagon, the White House and

State Department…and that Colonel, is why you've been assigned here, I asked for you. We need your expertise on our staff that's why we're having this conversation today. I also talked with your Ambassador boss at State and you come highly recommended. The reason for the sleight of hand and secret handshake is the job I've picked you for is an Army billet and sticking you in there now would really piss off all the Little Green Army Men. When the current Chief retires in the next month or so, we will quickly convert the job to an Air Force billet and slide you in. Until then, this conversation never happened, keep your lips sealed, if the word gets out you won't get the job. Tell no one including your wife, and congratulations to the soon to be new Chief of the Special Operations Division, J-36." You could have knocked Sluggo over with a feather, overjoyed to say the least, "I guess there really is a grand plan, and now I know who requested me and why I'm here."

So back to CCIP with a big s-eating grin on his face. Biding his time at CCIP…one day a Navy Captain (same as a Colonel in the AF) showed up in the office and said, "I'm going to be working here." Sluggo greeted him and they talked, he advised Sluggo that he was a Navy Cryptologist Officer…known in the Navy as a "Cryppy." Sluggo thought, "That makes sense, he would be the right flavor to take this job." The guy commented that two 0-6's in this job was overkill and rather unusual, he then noted that Sluggo was a pilot and asked him what his "date of rank" was. Sluggo in shock replied," I think it's around March something, I don't know the exact date." This date of rank thing is a big deal with the Navy…not so much with the Air Force. Sluggo thought, "This jerk wants to see if he outranks me so he can boss around the office. Obviously, he is my replacement, but he doesn't know it, and evidently the word about my demise as the CCIP Chief is not common knowledge…good. I feel sorry for my old CCIP crew working for this Crippy toad, they're a good group and he's kind of a prig."

Later that week, as Sluggo was walking down one of the halls (passageways in Navy speak), he ran into a Special Forces (Green Beret) Army LTC (call sign Jake) he had worked with in the past. Jake asked, "What brings you here Colonel?" probably thinking a no notice exercise or evaluation or something. Sluggo said, "Jake I'm assigned here now in CCIP." Jake said, "What's that?" and Sluggo explained and they both went their separate ways. He found out later that Jake ran back to his office and told his boys, "I ran into Sluggo, that AF Colonel from State, he's stationed here now and I have a strange feeling that he's going to end up being our new boss"...great intuition snake eater Jake, but what did you really say?

Sluggo thought, "Perhaps I should find an abode for Shooter and me to live in." The plan was to send a shipment of household goods now (December) and one when Shooter leaves (March) but he needed a place to send them. Sluggo went to the consolidated military housing office to get a house on base and found out there were many options at the many bases on the island, some very nice, some not so nice, some even on the water. "But for a Colonel house there is a waiting list and we can't predict when one will come open." "Better find a rental," Sluggo thought, and after much searching, he found a great place on the south end of the island on a hill on a point overlooking the ocean, standing in the back yard you couldn't see another house, only mountains and sea." It was a trip to Camp Smith, but worth the drive. The owner lived in Taiwan and wasn't coming back to Hawaii any time soon. It was affordable with two housing allowances so sign a year lease and move in. Buy a few essentials, bed, TV, microwave, chair, just the man cave basics, the furniture and stuff will be coming later.

One Saturday morning as Sluggo was watching the news, the weather guessers were reporting an evil snowstorm on the east coast, with about a foot in DC. He called his beloved Shooter and expressed his sorrow, she said she was shoveling away, and asked him what he was doing. His smart ass response, "I'm sitting in the back yard sipping a Mai Tai, it's a beautiful day here in paradise in low 80's with a wonderful sea breeze, sure wish you were here"…if NSA was monitoring the phone line, they might have learned a few new foul words. The idea was to meet Shooter in Oregon for Christmas with her doing the final move in early March. It was soon New Year's Eve, because of the time difference, Sluggo called Shooter early Hawaii time to wish her a great new year, he then had a few beverages, and went to sleep watching news years on the tube. A little after midnight he was awakened by explosions, it sounded like a war, Sluggo ran outside and the island was going wild with every firework known to man as far as the eye could see, rockets, crackers, roman candles, mortars, the works.

One of his neighbors was out in the street with a stepladder and a pole with a string of firecrackers about 30 feet long tied to the top, "It's 15,000 salutes, watch this" he said as he lit them. "Impressive," thought Sluggo, and the festivities went on for hours. Shooter needed to share this event, so regardless of the hour Sluggo called her and stuck the phone out the window for her to hear the mayhem, she said she was impressed, probably wasn't, "you had to be here," said Sluggo. High speed fireworks were officially outlawed on Oahu, but you could get a free permit at a fire station to buy 500 lady finger type crackers, but no aerial or big stuff. The black market, however, thrived with barge loads of everything pyrotechnic, and the enforcers looked the other way. In the morning, the gunpowder haze wafted over the whole island, all the streets were paved with red firecracker paper and expended aerial junk, and the smoke from several of the grass fires that happen every year floated through the air. Who knew that New Year's Eve in Hawaii was such a Blast? Shooter finally made it to paradise and life was good.

So, what's with Sluggo's new gig? Sluggo was assigned to the Director of Operations, J-3 as the Director of the Special Operations Division, J-36, working for a Marine two-star general with a one-star Air Force general as his deputy…both were pilots who could converse in

airplane speak. J-36 was about 20 strong with all services, Army Special Forces, Navy SEALs, Air Force, Marines and civilians, the division was also augmented by Reservists, so at any one time about 25 or more folks were in attendance. Sluggo's J-36 mission was an odd collection of responsibilities, Counterterrorism, Antiterrorism, Civil Affairs, Psychological Operations, and other dogs and cats…a happy band of snake eaters.

A key responsibility was the CINCPAC interface with the Special Operations Command Pacific (SOCPAC)…more about them later. Some of the other dogs and cats included Combat Camera, Law Enforcement Policy (cops), the Asia Pacific Defense Forum Magazine, and for administration purposes the Central Identification Laboratory Hawaii

(CILHI) accounting for POW/MIAs of the Vietnam and Korean wars. The J-36 position was also a jump billet…as in parachuting out of a perfectly good aircraft. Sluggo thought, "Twenty years ago that would have been great…I'm older and a little bit wiser, thanks for the offer but my idea of a good time is driving airplanes not leaping out of them."

Sluggo's boss was a crusty old Marine two-star fighter pilot and a great guy though short of stature. He was also a heavy smoker; above his office door was a large sign "Smoke 'em if you got 'em," scattered throughout his office were several of the classic large standup ashtrays…push a button and the ashes go away. His deputy was an equally crusty, very tall old AF one-star fighter pilot also a great guy, they were quite the Mutt and Jeff winning team. Sluggo was the first bomber pilot to darken their doorstep…ergo he took some mandatory grief…fighter pilot crap with lots of hand gestures…Sluggo parried with I can lose three engines and still flop around… fighter pilots and a bomber pilot united under the same roof…what a concept.

One of Sluggo's missions was to be the liaison and point of contact

between CINCPAC and the newly formed SOCPAC. SOCPAC was a sub-unified command, subordinate to USCINCPAC. They were activated at the end of 1983, a few years before Sluggo got there, with only eighteen headquarters personnel and their assigned units, Army Special Forces in Okinawa, SEALs and Air Force Special Ops in the Philippines. They were steadily growing with a one-star

commander and their headquarters based at Fort Shaftner, an Army base down the road from CINCPAC. They lived in a large WW II underground bunker named the tunnel. An important mission of SOCPAC was forming a highly capable joint crisis response force…this joint force was a rather new concept in the military.

The CINCPAC rapidly deployable unit was called Joint Task Force 510 (JTF-510). It was composed of SOCPAC guys and Sluggo's troops with the general in charge and Sluggo as his deputy. JTF-510 could deploy rapidly as an advance party to a crisis situation to provide situation assessments, to recommend courses of action, and/or to conduct military operations. JTF-510 provided humanitarian assistance, disaster relief, noncombatant evacuation, and other contingency support, including providing an in-extremist counterterrorist response force (shooters). More about JTF-510 later.

Part of Sluggo's mission was to administratively represent the

Central Identification Laboratory, Hawaii with CINCPAC. CILHI was the organization formed to recover and identify American Missing in Action (MIAs) remains following the Vietnam War (their role has since expanded to a worldwide mission including all conflicts). CILHI used military personnel from all branches of the military and civilian staff. Back in the day, their work involved sending recovery teams to suspected sites in Southeast Asia and conducting excavations for MIA remains. The remains were then flown to their laboratory in Hawaii where they underwent forensic identification to match the remains using DNA, dental, medical, military records and any other means to make a positive identification.

The CILHI Chief invited Sluggo down to his place for a meet and greet and a tour of the facility. Sluggo and several of his boys made the trip to Barbers Point, a Naval Air Station a few miles past Pearl Harbor where CILHI lived. Their lab was impressive, state of the art gear,

and forensic scientists conducting a detailed and exacting process. The Chief presented a briefing that outlined the process, step by step from finding the remains, recovering same and shipping back to Hawaii for the identification process. As an example, the Chief said, "We recently identified the remains of an F-105 fighter pilot from Oregon shot down over North Vietnam…and here's how we did it." As the Chief explained and outlined the documentation, Sluggo noticed the name of deceased. Sluggo felt as if he had been struck by a lightning bolt, the remains were from a buddy he had grown up with, grade school, high school, football and double dating, college and Air Force ROTC and drill team, a really great guy. A true epiphany for Sluggo. Everyone else was also stunned. Sluggo thought, "I knew he was MIA; I now toast to his honor and for finally being found."

Another of Sluggo's missions was point of contact and liaison with JSOC. JSOC was formed after the failed U.S. hostage rescue attempt, *Eagle*

Claw, 1980, in Iran. JSOC is charged to plan and conduct highly classified special operations exercises and training; to develop joint special operations tactics; and to execute special operations missions worldwide, deploy anywhere within hours. JSOC *Special Mission Units* that have been acknowledged, include *Army Operational Detachment-Delta* (Delta Force), *Naval Special Warfare Development Group* (DEVGUR- Seal Team 6), *Air Force Special Tactics Squadron*, and others, some remain classified. JSOC operations and units are often called *Black SOF*. Sluggo was readily acceptable and very useful to represent the otherwise aloof and secretive JSOC as he had worked closely with them during both his White House and State Department assignments…they knew him, and he was trusted.

A tragic event occurred in Philippines; A U.S. Army Colonel was murdered by terrorists on his way to work. The Colonel was assigned as the Chief of the Army division of the Joint U.S. Military Advisory Group (JUSMAG), providing counter-insurgency training and equipment for the Armed Forces of the Philippines (the Colonel was one of the few Army POWs that escaped from Viet Cong captivity during the war). JUSMAGs throughout the world are rather strange organizations, DoD personal working closely with the State Department through the U.S. Embassy in the country. The U.S. Military Attaché in the Embassy under the supervision of the American Ambassador is usually also the Chief of JUSMAG. Other than providing administrative support to JUSMAG military personnel, CINCPAC had no other real dealings with them.

The Colonel was working closely with the U.S. and Philippine intelligence agencies trying to penetrate the New People's Army (NPA), the communist insurgency that threatened to overthrow the Philippines' government. Violence and terrorism were commonplace throughout this period directed against U.S. personnel and facilities. The Colonel reported that he had acquired intelligence information which indicated that the communists were planning a major terrorist act. He warned his superiors that a high-profile figure was about to be assassinated and that he himself was second or third on the assassination list. One morning on his way to work in the JUSMAG compound outside of Manila, his car was attacked by insurgents. His vehicle, a lightly armored sedan was hit by twenty-one bullets, one round entered, penetrating the frame between the armored window and the car body. It was determined that was only area that a slug could have penetrated the armor. The round struck the Colonel in the head, killing him instantly, and wounding his chauffeur.

The State Department formed an Accountability Review Board (ARB) and deployed it to Manila. The General sent Sluggo with the ARB to determine if CINCPAC could have done anything to prevent the tragedy. They met at the Embassy, covered the route (in more heavily armored vehicles) where the incident occurred, and examined the security of the JUSMAG compound. It was determined that the attack was well planned and executed, and U.S. personnel were at risk traveling in vehicles. The whole structure of JUSMAG security and responsibilities needed to be changed. Sluggo briefed all the heavies back home that the Board determined that CINCPAC wasn't at fault and new security procedures were being written. The JUSMAG Chief in the Philippines, an Army one-star demanded new armored sedans ASAP. Surprisingly, the new vehicles were available and shipped to him quickly. Rumor had it that when they arrived, he emptied an M-16 on one to test the armor (did Sluggo see the pictures?)...it passed.

It wasn't all work and no play at mother CINCPAC. Many Friday afternoon staff meetings; sanity checks, were usually held in beautiful and peaceful outdoors surroundings, fore. On a Marine Camp, working for a Marine General, the Corps birthday was a national holiday and the Marine Corps Ball was a mandatory military formation...and lots of fun.

Shooter finally pinned on her gold Major leaves and started a new job, Air Force Element Commander. The Element was responsible for providing AF administrative support for all Air Force personnel assigned to joint jobs throughout the Pacific, embassies, JUSMAGs, other commands, intelligence functions, etc. It was a command position...not bad for a Major and technically she was Sluggo's AF boss. Sluggo came to work one morning and was informed by the Air Force Element that he had been selected for random drug testing, peeing in the bottle, always a great event. So, go do it, no problem and back to work. A month or so later, another test required, again the next month. Sluggo thought soon I won't be able to pee without someone watching. Since the requests were coming from Shooter's AF Element, Sluggo detected an elephant in the room...preferential treatment...or abuse. When confronted, Shooter remarked with a snide grin "Don't you know that we need to test our share of Colonels, but I can assure you that selection is a very random process." Sluggo remarked, "I'm not buying that bridge you're trying to sell me," answered by another Shooter grin, plausible deniability.

Sluggo's crusty old Air Force one-star Deputy J-3 was retiring, he was a good guy and no one wanted to see him go. The rumor was in the wind that the Air Force was cutting back on senior officers. "Just another thing to worry about," thought Sluggo. The General's replacement was a newly weaned, baby Air Force one-star, a serious-minded mathematician fighter pilot...quite a change from crusty. During his initial one-on-one, meet and greet with Sluggo, he asked "How does an AF bomber driver end up as the Division Chief of Special Operations?" Sluggo explained and thought, "I'll have to clean up my act and I don't think he digs snake eaters." Turned out he was in the Pentagon as a Colonel when Sluggo was there although their paths had never crossed.

The General's wife was quite proper and wanted to become involved socially as the first wife, so she proposed, and the General agreed, that a social program was in order with the Colonels and Navy Captains that worked for her husband and all their wives... and it was to be called, "The Gathering of Eagles." The first event was scheduled on a Saturday evening, a social and sit-down dinner in a private room in the very nice Hickam AF Base Officers Club. The menu would include her family favorite chicken with garlic sauce, and for dessert another world-famous family favorite, bread pudding with vanilla sauce. The General's wife went so far as to meet with the chef with tips to ensure the food would be made properly. The night came to be with about 20 0-6s and wives. The social hour went well with tasty nibblers and all sat down for the dinner. The proper blessing and appropriate toasts were made, and the main course was served piping hot by the chef and his worker bees. The chicken tasted different but not bad. Soon it was dessert time, the bread pudding was served with the hot sauce ladled on top. After the first bite or two, there was a pregnant pause as everyone looked around at fellow diners. There was a gasp from the General's wife and her face turned red...and you guessed it, the chicken had been served with the vanilla sauce and the dessert with the garlic sauce. Future "Gathering of Eagles' did not include a sit-down dinner featuring family favorites.

Sluggo got a secure conference call from JSOC and his old terrorism office at State. They were proposing a joint briefing trip (State, military, intelligence, FBI) throughout the Pacific for U.S. Ambassadors and senior Embassy staff on counterterrorism response and assistance and what to expect if an incident was to happen on their turf. The plan was to cover eight U.S. Embassies in about a two-week period and they wanted Sluggo to represent CINCPAC and brief the assistance that they could provide as JSOC was on its way (the Pacific is a great big place). Sluggo briefed his bosses, they gave him their blessing and the planning began.

The countries purposed were the Philippines, Papua New Guinea, Indonesia, Malaysia, Sri Lanka, Thailand, and India. They would have their own airplane, an Air Force C-22, military version of the B-727 medium range airliner based at Andrews AFB. It was to be flown by three USAF JSOC crews with a secondary mission being orientation of civilian airports not commonly visited by the military  and whatever other useful intel they could pick along the way. The C-22 was not a long-range aircraft so they would island hop across the Pacific. The airplane was a good choice for the places they were going, very reliable, could use small airports and shorter runways, and with built-in rear air-stairs (of D. B. Cooper hijacking and bailout fame) and required little ground support.

Finally, everything was good to go with all the Embassies and everyone else concurred, no mean feat. The Air Force agreed as long as they would take "space available" military folks when possible. So, the event began Andrews AFB to Travis AFB to Hickam AFB to pick up Sluggo, no more space A passengers from this point on. A stop at Wake Island for gas. Wake was an interesting place besides being a testimony to early aviation and heroic U.S. WW II action, it had a nearly 10,000' runway, one of the longest in the Pacific. Wake is administered by the

 USAF under an agreement with the U.S. Department of Interior. The commander was an AF Major with an NCO deputy and 100 Thai workers that ran the airport and the island. All the comforts of home built up during the Vietnam War where it was a busy place, nearly new housing, exchange and commissary all ranks club and outstanding modern airfield capabilities most shut down and empty. It was used only for transiting aircraft emergencies and military aircraft refueling stops, prior permission required. Sluggo thought, "What a wonderful place to use for a counterterrorism staging base and exercises, I'll keep that in mind." So,

refuel and tour the island (didn't take long) then off to the next stop Guam and old memories for Sluggo.

The rule now was no uniforms, shorts and tee shirts please. The motley crew was made up of about 20; some aircrew, some briefers and a few snake eaters thrown in for good measure. The airplane was very comfortable with about 30 first class airline seats, a working area with tables and full airline galley. Since they were staying a day on Guam, the plan was to hit the commissary and load up on food and beverages (beer authorized) before heading out for the great unknown.

There are many great stories related to this trip, here's a few. The first briefing stop was Manila, Sluggo knew the Embassy folks there well and had been there numerous times, the briefing went great. Off to the next stop Port Moresby, Papua New Guinea. None of the boys had been there before and they didn't know what to expect, the Embassy set up rooms at a downtown hotel and picked them up at the airport. The hotel was part of an Australian chain, fairly new and modern (Aussies seemed run the show in PNG). As they were checking in, the Aussie clerk informed them they had missed all the action as the hotel had been robbed the day before by a local man armed with a machete, the weapon of choice on the island. He explained that a new and powerful local brew was just released and some of the natives were going a bit loony. He said if they wanted to really harm you, they would use the sharpened edge of the blade, if not, the flat of the blade...he also suggested they stay in the hotel and not wander around downtown. Get some sleep, brief the Ambassador in the morning, back to the airport and depart, next stop Darwin Australia.

The next leg would be tight on fuel, so they decided to stop in Darwin, gas up quickly and depart. Darwin airport shared the runway with the Royal Australian Air Force (RAAF) so it should be a short stop. After landing they were met by Australian Officials whom thought it rather odd that a strange USAF airplane that they had never seen before was manned by some chaps dressed like the Beach Boys. The RAAF troops said it would be three or four hours before they could refuel as they were having an inspection. Customs said you have to stick close to the terminal (shared with the civilian side) so they had some lunch and a beer. The terminal bar was like the Old West, wild looking characters firing down the many drinks before their flights.

The guys checked with the RAAF and they said it would be several more hours. They asked if there was any place around where they could buy some cases of Fosters, Aussies finest beer. They said there was a package store just off base and offered to give the boys a ride to pick some up. A couple of the gang went, bought three or four cases of Fosters, and started to return. As they made their way back, they got stopped at the gate for an ID check, (remember the inspection). They got caught and explained who they were and what they were doing. The cop said, "I should arrest you, but since you were just buying some Foster's I'll let you go, have a nice flight and this time stay close to the terminal." Busted in Darwin, what a hoot. Self- catered food and drink on the airplane was a great idea, they tried to stock up on goodies at the embassies or wherever whenever they could. The Darwin refueling was done and so were the boys, so let's depart for the next stop Jakarta, Indonesia.

Jakarta was very nice, they got some sleep, the briefing went well then off to the next stop, Kuala Lampur, Malaysia and another successful brief. Since Islam was the dominate religion in both countries, the Moslem influence was most interesting and noticeable. Next stop Colombo, Sri Lanka. The embassy in Colombo had a greater sense of urgency as a civil war was going full speed and the Tamil Tigers were running amok. Wheels up, next stop New Deli, India.

The size of India was impressive as they droned across it for what seemed like days. They landed at night and taxied to the military ramp where the airplane would be "guarded." The ride to the hotel was an adventure, some kind of holiday was going on and the smoke and smog was thick, the trip was also interrupted when they had to maneuver to avoid hitting a sacred cow. Upon arriving at the nice, new, modern hotel, the clerk informed them in no way should they drink the water, only drink the bottled water from the front deck. If there was "bottled water" in the rooms, it was just tap water as the maids had probably made off with the real stuff and just refilled the bottles from the tap. Good brief at the Embassy then off to Bangkok, Thailand. At the airport as they neared their jet, they noticed their "guard" an old Indian man in traditional garb sitting on bench, resting his eyes with a vintage WW II Sten Gun laying across his lap.

Bangkok was the last embassy brief on the trip, Sluggo hadn't been there since the 70's…what a change, from sleepy hollow to big city blues. Embassy brief great…work well done, mission accomplished. The guys took the next day off, some shopping perhaps, lots of room on the airplane. Sluggo wondered if Venus Jewelers was still there, it was and away they went… greeted there by a "we remember you" and they pulled out some old picture albums and there was Sluggo's BUFF crew clowning for the camera. Venus lived up to their nickname "Venus Cleaners" and the guys left with lots of good stuff and were cleaned out of all their Bhat. Homeward bound, Philippines, Guam, Wake Island, Honolulu…What A Trip.

Civil Affairs and Psychological Operations (PSYOPS) were important parts of Special Operations, both specialties were primarily U.S. Army Reserve positions. Civil Affairs provide interface between the military and civil authorities and civilian populations especially during contingency operations such as disaster relief. PSYOPS operations provide information

to the public favorable to the U.S./military. His Reservists were an important asset of Sluggo's organization and JTF-510. From 1989-1993 CINCPAC provided direct military assistance to relief operations during 22 foreign and domestic natural disasters including cyclones, typhoons, earthquakes and even a volcano

eruption in the Philippines. That much activity stressed the active duty forces (Sluggo and Shooter spent many a moon in the Command Center) and using Reservists to augment was critical. Since JTF-510 was self-contained and could deploy short notice they were always under the gun.

A reserve story, one of Sluggo's Army Reserve LTC, a big guy and former Olympic class bicycle rider, got promoted to Colonel. He came to Sluggo's office bright and early the next morning proudly wearing his new rank. Sluggo checked him out and something didn't look quite right, so he discretely pulled him aside and told him that his colonel eagles were on backwards. He turned red and explained that his buddies told him that traditionally, the eagles' heads were supposed to look back to see if the enemy was sneaking up on you. Sluggo said, "I think that you've been screwed, blued and tattooed by your good buddies, and you might remind them paybacks are hell."

Counterterrorism exercises were the flavor of the week and Sluggo and his gang were in it up to their ears in them, Oahu, the Big Island, Johnson Island, Kwajalein Atoll, Wake Island, (his SEALS nearly drowned Sluggo in the surf at a post exercise party on Wake), Guam, Philippines, Thailand, and other garden spots in paradise, you get the idea.

SSBN 732

Sluggo wondered if he could use submarines in his exercises so he asked and to his surprise he was invited to go on one for a sail or cruise or dive or whatever you call it. The Navy had converted one of the older

SSBM's to support SEAL Special Operations, complete with a dry deck shelter on its back with a SEAL Delivery Vehicle (mini sub) inside. That boat was in maintenance so Sluggo left Pearl Harbor on the USS Alaska a fairly new SSBN for the cooks tour, crawl all over the boat, fancy lunch in the wardroom, dive, dive, dive, surface, then cruise down Waikiki in the coning tower. "Very cool" thought Sluggo "I've got to have one of these but day cruises only…when this thing takes off its gone for months."

JSOC was deploying DEVGRU (SEALS) to Hawaii for a hush hush exercise with Sluggo's old office at State. One Sunday morning, Sluggo got a call from the Command Center asking if he knew anything about the fancy trucks with Virginia plates manned by macho men pulling high speed go-fast boats down Ala Moana Blvd. in Waikiki, Sluggo replied "Yes, but I can't talk about it on this phone, but really it's no big deal, I've got it covered"… that seemed to sooth the Command Center folks. "So much for Operational Security (OPSEC)" thought Sluggo, "thank goodness it's the weekend."

Back to Camp H.M. Smith, if you recall the wooden buildings were thrown together during WW II and after 40 plus years were in sad shape. Termites are known to be very active on all the Hawaiian Islands. Formosan Termites love to eat wood and are known to swarm at night. When Shooter first got to the Camp, her office was inside a security vault area because of the classified computer systems that lived there. Across the hall were the nuke warfare folks also inside a vault. Early one Monday morning when Shooter got to work all hell was breaking loose in the vaults. One of the nuke guys classified containers...500 pound safe...had fallen through the floor and was now residing in the office below. Soviet termites suspected, but it appears no classified documents were eaten.

It was the end of the year and December 7th was fast approaching, it was also the 50th anniversary of the bombing of Pearl Harbor and the

President was coming to town to officiate. Being a former Navy aviator and staffer who had served there both as a bomber pilot and intelligence officer at Makalapa during the war, the island military were to be key players, and since Sluggo and his guys were counterterrorism and law enforcement, long hours were ahead. Among other fears, it was estimated

that if a serious incident occurred, the island cellphone system would crash. Sluggo suggested that satellite radios be positioned at each location where the President would appear. "Great idea" said his General, "make it happen Sluggo." "Me and my big

mouth" thought our boy as portable SATCOMs were scarce and in high demand, but he made it happen as he begged borrowed and stole radios from everywhere. Since tensions in the Middle East were on a high, security was tight including SEALs in the water around the USS Arizona Memorial. No fear, all festivities went perfectly.

A few months later, the Air Force Thunderbirds were coming to town and would perform over the beach on Waikiki. One of the CINCPAC guys was a former Thunderbird (AF precision flying team) so a party was in order. He rented a big corner suite at the top

of the Hawaiian Village, floor to ceiling windows and balconies. The great day came and about 15 or more couples assembled to watch the show and party. Since the jets were over water, they could go low and at times were below the level of the room. The crew gathered on the balconies, the view was fantastic at one point, one of the wives looked into the room and about half of the guys including Sluggo were in the room watching out of the windows. She said, "Come out on the balconies there's plenty of room." The guys said, "We're OK in here." You guessed it, they were all pilots and didn't care for heights...the boys took mega grief for that display of courage.

The war drums of Saddam Hussen were beating louder by the day in Iraq, the Soviets good buddy and state sponsor of terrorism was loudly rattling his scimitar. Iraq was deep in debt following the war with Iran. They owed Kuwait and Saudi Arabia big bucks...and they both had scads of oil. "Kuwait has been stealing our oil and has the access to the Gulf that I need," thought Saddam, also "they have a piddling little military and I have a mighty one, I think I'll invade, "so he did. Within 12 hours, most resistance had ended within Kuwait, and the royal family had fled, leaving Iraq in control of most of Kuwait. After two days of intense combat, most of the Kuwaiti military were either overrun by the Iraqi Republican Guard or had escaped to Saudi Arabia. Following Kuwait's conquest, the Iraqi Army was within easy striking distance of Saudi oil fields. Control of these fields, along with Kuwaiti and Iraqi reserves, would have given Saddam control over the majority of the world's oil reserves. Iraq also had a number of grievances with Saudi Arabia. The Saudis had lent Iraq some 26 billion dollars during its war with Iran. The Saudis had backed Iraq in that war, as they feared the influence of Shia Iran's Islamic revolution on its own Shia minority. After the war, Saddam felt he should not have to repay the loans due to the help he had given the Saudis by fighting Iran. Is an attack on Saudi coming soon? The West was highly concerned. A 34-nation coalition was formed, objective; free Kuwait and destroy Saddam's military. And so, it began as the world watched on TV.

Things at CINCPAC were on a fever pitch; the Ops Center up and running 24/7, and JTF-510 was on a hair trigger to deploy. Sluggo's boss said, "Get your ass out there and make sure that the counterterrorist forces are linked in communication and ready to go." Sluggo set out to visit the Army SF and Marine Corps Special Operations Training Group (SOTG) in Okinawa and SEALs and Air Force SF in the Philippines (the Marine SOTG had been recently added to complement JTF-510, one of Sluggo's former Marines was the commander).

Sluggo made his way to Hickam AFB as a C-5 was soon to depart for Kadena AB via Guam. About two hours into the flight the jet's air conditioning went to full hot and couldn't be controlled, the plastic insulation got very hot and a nasty odor filled the passenger compartment, the crew passed out wet rags for the passengers to cover their noses, descended below 10,000 feet turned the pressurization off, declared an emergency and returned to Hawaii. "Not a great start," thought Sluggo.

There was a KC-135 tanker soon to depart for Okinawa and Sluggo climbed aboard, after engine start, they detected a fuel leak before they left parking..."That jet is not going anywhere soon" thought Sluggo, "perhaps Mr. Murphy is telling me something." Next stop a C-130 leaving that day for Guam then Kadena. Sluggo was beat up and sick of airplanes by the time he got to Okinawa...but he got there. A few days meeting with the troops, all was well, SATCOMs working great, no discernable terrorism threat to Okinawa.

Time to head to the Philippines and the SEALs and Air Force SO. There had just been a terrorist incident in the Philippines. Two Iraqi intelligence agents, Ahmed and Kahim plotted to bomb the U.S. Thomas Jefferson Cultural Center in Manila. They made their way to plant a PETN improvised explosive device (IED) in a big canvas bag against the building. Ahmed began to set the timer, Kahim said, "Ahmed, I think you're winding it the wrong way"...oops...too late...detonation. Ahmed was killed instantly by the blast, and his body absorbed most of the impact, a wounded Kahim wandered dazed, covered in his colleague's guts through the street until a cab driver noticed him and brought him to a hospital and subsequent arrest. The police later found Ahmed's foot up in a tree. Similar failed attacks happened in Indonesia and Thailand...the Iraqi spooks weren't doing so well in the Pacific. All was well with the SEALs and the AF, communication links were up and ready to go. Sluggo spend a few days with the troops, took a couple of HH-3 Jolly Green helicopter rides, drank a few San Miguel beers and finally made his way back to Hawaii and home...what a trip.

"Tempus Fugit, time flies"...especially when you're having fun. The end of Sluggo's Hawaii tour was rapidly approaching, he had worn the joint purple suit (not pure AF Blue) for 10 or so years, he wasn't going to make General, no command or flying jobs on the horizon, the AF didn't know what to do with him, Shooter however, had a fast moving career ahead and a school slot to Staff College in Alabama. Must be time to retire. Sluggo mused, "The last 27 years were the greatest, I wouldn't change much, I've had some super jobs, seen the government in action from the military through the executive branch and in between. Flying the BUFF was the bee's knees, I'll never forget it. Leading the Special Operations crew at CINCPAC was a blast. Met wonderful people, some true friends for life...a great ride for an Irish lad from Mallory Avenue in Portland Oregon, you couldn't have made this stuff up if you tried." J-3 and his guys sent him off with great fanfare. Green pastures of shamrocks ahead...in Alabama, "Sure, you bet, there's no stinking shamrocks in Alabama."

Caption: King of Malaysia at Royal Fleet Review; Governor of Penang at Royal Fleet Review; Grand Poohbah of Spec Ops at Royal Golf Review

Sleep well, your AIR FORCE is awake!!!!!!!!

This is the end of the Sluggo Chronicles, Memoirs of an Old Bomber Pilot; further civilian Chronicles might be forthcoming.... only Sluggo knows.

ABOUT THE AUTHOR

Patrick F. Daly, Colonel, USAF (Ret.) entered the Air Force in 1965 as a graduate from the ROTC program at the University of Portland, Portland, Oregon. He completed Undergraduate Pilot Training in 1967 and flew the B-52 at Fairchild and Castle Air Force Bases; a Command Pilot with over 5,000 hours in Models C thru H including 426 Arc Light/Bullet Shot missions and over 2,300 combat hours. His final flying job was Bomber Branch Chief, Central Flight Instructor Course at Castle. Other military assignments included Chief, Contingency Support Branch, Headquarters USAF, the Pentagon, Vice President's Task Force on Combatting Terrorism, The White House, Senior Military Advisor to the Ambassador at Large for Counterterrorism, Department of State, and Chief, Special Operations Division, U.S. Pacific Command. He became active in combatting terrorism policy while at the Pentagon, after retiring from the Air Force he held several senior counterterrorism positions at the Department of Energy and the National Nuclear Security Administration. He retired from Federal Service in 2012 and remains active as a senior counterterrorism policy consultant. He was awarded the Defense Superior Service Medal, Legion of Merit, Distinguished Flying Crosses, Meritorious Service Medals, Air Medals, the Distinguished Career Service Award, and other military and civilian awards.